National Council of Teachers of English
Research Report No. 13

The Composing Processes
of Twelfth Graders

NCTE Research Report No. 13

The Composing Processes *of Twelfth Graders

ANET EMIG

Rutgers, the State University of New Jersey

ational Council of Teachers of English
111 Kenyon Road, Urbana, Illinois 61801

NCTE COMMITTEE ON RESEARCH James R. Squire, Ginn and Company, Chairman/Doris V. Gunderson, U.S Office of Education, Associate Chairman/Thomas C. Barrett, University of Wisconsin/Nathan S. Blount, University of Wisconsin/John R. Bormuth, University of Chicago/Earl W. Buxton University of Alberta/James Hoetker, University of Illinois/ Stanley B. Kegler, University of Minnesota/Geraldine E. LaRocque, Teachers College, Columbia University/Evan Glyn Lewis, University of Wales/Roy C. O'Donnell, Florida State University/Walter T. Petty, State University of New York at Buffalo/Alan C. Purves, University of Illinois/Mildred E. Riling, Southeastern State College, Oklahoma/ William D. Sheldon, Syracuse University/J. Stephen Sherwin, State University of New York at Buffalo/Robert F. Hogan, NCTE *ex officio/* Bernard O'Donnell, NCTE/ERIC *ex officio*/CONSULTANT READERS FOR THIS MANUSCRIPT Earl W. Buxton, University of Alberta/J. Stephen Sherwin, State University of New York at Buffalo/COMMITTEE ON PUBLICATIONS Robert F. Hogan, NCTE Executive Secretary, Chairman/ Robert Dykstra, University of Minnesota/Walker Gibson, University of Massachusetts, Amherst/Robert E. Palazzi, Burlingame High School, California/Eugene C. Ross, NCTE Director of Publications/EDITORIAL SERVICES Nancy Beach, NCTE Headquarters/BOOK DESIGN Norma Phillips Meyers, NCTE Headquarters

Library of Congress Catalog Card Number 77-163358
ISBN 0-8141-0803-2
NCTE Stock Number 08032

This report describes an expedition into new territory, an investigation of the writing *process*. This is an area hitherto almost untouched by researchers in written composition who by and large have focused their attention upon the *written product*.

Over the years, this sustained concentration upon using data gathered from an analysis of what students have written has contributed to our understanding of the ways that writing competence is affected by such factors as linguistic environment, student maturation, the teaching of grammars, the practice of writing "a theme a week," and various kinds of instruction. However, an analysis of the product, even when it involves using some of the transformational instruments designed by recent investigators, does not provide answers to a question that has loomed large in most discussions of contemporary education. This question is concerned with what happens to the student's *self* as a result of the educational process. This is the question for which Professor Emig is seeking answers in her investigation of "the ways that students usually or typically behave as they write." In essence, she is attempting to identify the student's feelings, attitudes, and self-concepts which form the invisible components of the "composition" that the teacher perceives as an arrangement of words, sentences, and paragraphs to be read, criticized, and evaluated.

Readers will find the Emig report lucid, scholarly, provocative, and at times disconcertingly outspoken. It is introduced by a refreshing discussion of the creative process in the world outside the classroom. This material, garnered from a comprehensive survey of the letters, memoirs, prefaces, critical essays, autobiographies, and recorded conversations of established writers, ranges from Plato's *Ion* to Auden's televised description of "The Creative Person."

Because her examination of students' writing behavior is an audacious venture into relatively unexplored territory, Professor Emig was forced to chart her own course. Her approach involved creating her own adaptation of the case-study method suggested by the editors of *Research in Written Composition*.[1] Her data are drawn from tape recordings of the comments made by eight twelfth-grade students who were asked to compose aloud; that is, to express orally the thoughts and feelings that came to them while they were engaged in writing three short themes during individual sessions with the investigator. Additional

---

1. Richard Braddock, Richard Lloyd-Jones, and Lowell Schoer, *Research in Written Composition* (Champaign, Ill.: National Council of Teachers of English, 1963).

information was provided by a "writing autobiography," a tape-recorded interview in which each of these students revealed his or her recollections of earlier writing experiences that proved either stimulating or traumatic. For example, one intelligent, sensitive eighteen-year-old recalled vividly the embarrassment suffered because of a spelling error she made in a composition written on the blackboard for a visiting superintendent when she was in fourth grade.

The information which emerges from Professor Emig's tightly structured analysis of these data will prove interesting—and perhaps disturbing—to teachers of written composition. For example, she finds several significant contradictions between what good students and established writers actually *do* and what language textbooks say that student writers *ought to do* during the composition process. She notes how students are concerned with applying their teachers' instructions, directives, admonitions, and criticisms. She examines the ways that "school-sponsored" and "self-sponsored" writing may influence the student's choice of topic, his selection of materials, his inclination toward "deep personal engagement" in his writing, and the attention which he devotes to planning, prewriting, and revision.

A perceptive investigator, Professor Emig points out that because of the limitations imposed by the size of her groups, the restricted number of pieces of writing, the presence of the investigator during the writing sessions, and the process of composing aloud, some of her conclusions must be considered tentative pending further research. Other investigators may find her methodology applicable not only to the replications she suggests, but to studies of pupil response to different kinds of writing instruction. For example, in their report on the teaching of English in the United Kingdom,[2] Squire and Applebee describe writing programs quite different from those observed in American secondary schools during an earlier survey.[3] A productive study might involve exposing two groups of students to the two kinds of program, and then using or modifying Professor Emig's "composing aloud" and "autobiographical" techniques to find out whether the different kinds of instruction appear to engender in students different writing behaviors, different attitudes toward composition, and different concepts of themselves.

Earl W. Buxton

For the Committee on Research

---

2. James R. Squire and Roger K. Applebee, *Teaching English in the United Kingdom* (Champaign, Ill.: National Council of Teachers of English, 1969).
3. James R. Squire and Roger K. Applebee, *High School English Instruction Today* (New York: Appleton-Century-Crofts, 1968).

TABLE OF CONTENTS

TABLES

PROTOCOLS

ACKNOWLEDGMENTS

I thank John Mellon, Wayne O'Neil, and Douglas Porter of the Harvard Graduate School of Education for reading the original manuscript.

I appreciate the thorough and perceptive comments made about the revised manuscript by Earl W. Buxton, J. Stephen Sherwin, and James R. Squire of the NCTE Committee on Research. I also appreciate the editorial assistance of Nancy Beach, NCTE Publications Department, as well as the thoughtful suggestions sent me by Sister M. Philippa Coogan, B.V.M., of the NCTE Commission on Composition.

I am grateful to Opie White for typing the original manuscript.

Without the cooperation of the eight vital, open, delightful participants there would, of course, have been no study.

My own teachers of composition down the years were splendidly different from the teachers I describe in this research report. I dedicate this report to them as representatives of all those teachers we remember with gratitude:

Lenore Davison, Williams Avenue Grade School, Norwood, Ohio

Wilma Hutchison, Walnut Hills High School, Cincinnati, Ohio

Lenore Branch, Joseph Bottkol, Marianne Brock, Joyce Horner, and Alan McGee, Mount Holyoke College, South Hadley, Massachusetts

Roy Cowden, University of Michigan, Ann Arbor

Priscilla Tyler, Harvard Graduate School of Education, Cambridge, Massachusetts.

New Brunswick, New Jersey   J. E.
September 1971

INTRODUCTION

Composing in writing is a common activity of literate persons. Yet descriptions of what occurs during this experience, not to mention attempts to explain or analyze, are highly unsatisfactory. An investigator who attempts to characterize the composing process fully and accurately finds that the sources available are too disheveled and contradictory to provide a coherent characterization.

About the only unanimity among the data is the assumption, in the words of D. Gordon Rohman, that "writing is usefully described as a process, something which shows continuous change in time like growth in organic nature."[1]*

Clearly, a single shared assumption can scarcely be regarded as an adequate amount of information to possess about so major a process as composing, a process that is not only experienced personally by so many, but presented to most students in the schools, from the elementary grades through the most advanced stages of graduate study. The secondary curriculum, for example, requires students to write, not only in English classes but in almost every other class as well; and students are frequently, and justly, reminded that skill in writing is a major determinant in college admission and, indeed, in the range of choices their personal and professional lives will proffer.

Also, teachers of English and of other subject-matters regularly engage in activities they characterize as "teaching composition," in which they make statements and give directives about how to write. Yet if certain elements in a certain order characterize the evolution of all student writing, or even most writing in a given mode, and very little is known about these elements or their ordering, the teaching of composition proceeds for both students and teachers as a metaphysical or, at best, a wholly intuitive endeavor.

The purpose of this inquiry† is to examine the composing process of twelfth-grade writers, using a case study method. Case study has scarcely been employed as a technique for securing data about the composing process of students, although so basic a means of systemat-

---

* Notes appear by chapter, beginning on page 137.

† The study presented here is a revision of the author's doctoral dissertation, completed at Harvard University in 1969.

ically collecting information seems not only inherently interesting but requisite to most sorts of future empirical investigations in this unexamined field.

Case study has long been a mode of inquiry within the physical, biological, and social sciences: powerful modern instances can be cited, for example, from psychiatry and from education. From his earliest papers Freud built his theory of personality upon the foundation of case study.[2] In contemporary psychiatry, Bruno Bettelheim uses a combined method of introspection and case study within such accounts of normal and deviant behavior as *Love Is Not Enough, The Informed Heart,* and *The Empty Fortress.*

Reading, a subdiscipline of education, has often proceeded via case study, particularly in its approach to remedial reading. Perhaps the best-known example here is *Why Pupils Fail in Reading* by Helen M. Robinson. Studies of initial language acquisition—by a generous definition, another subdiscipline of education—also employ case studies. *The Language and Thought of the Child* by Jean Piaget examines the verbal behavior of Pie and Lev, two six-year-olds, as a source of hypotheses about the interactions of thought and language within children.

Reviewers of research in composition recommend the use of the case-study approach. In his 1963 review, Henry Meckel suggests that case studies may be useful in ascertaining possible relationships between language and personality:

> In a certain sense, the language patterns and style of a person may be regarded as an intrinsic part of his personality. There is great need, therefore, for case studies that will throw light on the relationship of different facets of personality to writing behavior, particularly on the dynamics of such relationships on dominant patterns of personality involved.[3]

More recently (1965), the editors of *Research in Written Composition* also suggest the probable values of a case-study approach to illuminate the psychological dimension of student writing—this despite, or because of, the fact that none of the 504 studies cited in their review of the research incorporates a case-study approach:

> The Van Bruggen study,* among others, suggests to the writers of this report that the psychological dimension of writing needs to be investigated by case-study procedures. Individual differences may "cancel out" in studies using the mean as the measure of the group. Case studies have

---

* See footnote on page 19.

done much to help remedial reading specialists understand and assist their "clients," and the similar complexities of writing suggest that much may be gained by developing case study procedures, against a background of experimental group research, to investigate the factors affecting the learning of composition and the procedures which will accelerate and maintain learning.[4]

Apparently only two extended efforts to use case study in examining student writing have been made. In 1961 an English writer, David Holbrook, published in *English for the Rejected* all the writing produced by nineteen "C-" and "D-stream" students whom he taught in a Cambridgeshire school. His analyses of their writing, accompanied by thumbnail prognoses for their future mental health by a psychiatrist, qualify as one of these efforts. The other is *36 Children* (1967), in which an American teacher, Herbert Kohl, describes, less fully and systematically, much of the writing done by the sixth-grade children in his Harlem classroom.

The series of case studies represented by the body of this research report seems then a legitimate, and needed, tapping of this mode of inquiry into the composing processes of students.

Twelfth-grade writers were chosen as a sample because, as the oldest members of the educational sequence experienced by most American youth, ostensibly they have experienced the widest range of composition teaching presented by our schools.

Eight twelfth graders of above average and average ability were asked, in four sessions each, to give autobiographies of their writing experiences and to compose aloud three themes in the presence of a tape recorder and the investigator.

Four hypotheses were formulated about their accounts and their writing behaviors:

1. Twelfth-grade writers engage in two modes of composing—reflexive and extensive—characterized by processes of different lengths with different clusterings of components.

2. These differences can be ascertained and characterized through having twelfth-grade writers compose aloud—that is, attempting to externalize their processes of composing.

3. In the composing processes of twelfth-grade writers, an implied or an explicit set of stylistic principles governs the selection and arrangement of components—lexical, syntactic, rhetorical, imagaic.

4. For twelfth-grade writers extensive writing occurs chiefly as a school-sponsored activity; reflexive, as a self-sponsored activity.

The crucial distinction in this study is between what are presented here as the two dominant modes of composing among older secondary-school students: the reflexive and the extensive. The reflexive mode is defined here as the mode that focuses upon the writer's thoughts and feelings concerning his experiences; the chief audience is the writer himself; the domain explored is often the affective; the style is tentative, personal, and exploratory. The extensive mode is defined here as the mode that focuses upon the writer's conveying a message or a communication to another; the domain explored is usually the cognitive; the style is assured, impersonal and often reportorial.

The data reveal that for American secondary school students in this sample, the sponsorship of these two modes of composing is divided, with extensive writing occurring chiefly as the school-sponsored mode; and with reflexive writing occurring chiefly as a self-sponsored activity of students.

The data also reveal that the composing process for the reflexive and the extensive modes differs in length and in the clustering of components. The process of reflexive, or self-sponsored, writing (in the United States, the equation seems legitimate), is a longer process with more portions; students writing reflexively often engage in quite long prewriting activities; they reformulate more; starting and stopping are more discernible moments in the process; and the aesthetic contemplation of their own product of writing sometimes occurs.

This study asked twelfth graders to compose aloud. Perhaps the characterization of this highly specialized form of verbal behavior is one of the most important contributions of this inquiry. Although the data are not full enough to substantiate any generalizations, they suggest, for future studies, an intensive examination of this behavior, especially the amounts of time needed for various kinds of grammatical and rhetorical transforming operations in composing.

The data strongly imply that changes need to be made in the way composition is taught in American secondary schools. A basic part of the revision is probably the training and retraining of teachers in composition: specifically, teachers of composition should themselves write in both the reflexive and the extensive mode so that when they teach, they are more likely to extend a wider range of writing invitations to their students.

It is important to note that this report does not claim to be a definitive, exhaustive, nor psychometrically-sophisticated account of how all twelfth graders compose. First, the sample of students, as well as the sample of writing they produced for this investigation, is far too small and skewed. Second, even the most mature and introspective students in the sample found composing aloud, the chief means the study employed for externalizing behavior, an understandably difficult, artificial, and at times distracting procedure. Third, the writer did not attempt to correlate the data collected with any outside, "objective" measures of writing ability—for example, the Sequential Test of Educational Progress (STEP) in Composition or the Student Aptitude Test (SAT) of the Educational Testing Service. Interesting correlations might also have been obtained by giving the students in the sample one or more tests of creativity, such as the Torrance Minnesota Tests of Creative Thinking and the Getzels-Jackson Battery on Creativity and Intelligence.

Having said all this, the writer wishes to reiterate what she believes are the values of this study. First, it represents a unique effort to utilize case studies for eliciting data about how students behave as they write. An experiment in capturing a process in process, the study provides certain kinds of data—humanistic data—that other kinds of inquiries into composition have not yet elicited. Perhaps its chief value is its steady assumption that persons, rather than mechanisms, compose.

In a speech as late as 1965, Kellogg Hunt characterized the state of our knowledge about the language of children as alchemy.[5] Alchemy is, equally, an apt metaphor to characterize the current state of our knowledge about how children—indeed, persons of all ages—compose. The writer's hope and ambition for this study is that it may provide one rung of a ladder up from alchemy, so the learning and the teaching of composition may someday attain the status of science as well as art.

CHAPTER 1

THE COMPOSING PROCESS: REVIEW OF THE LITERATURE

Most of the data about the composing process occur as three broad types. First there are accounts concerning established writers, chiefly of imaginative, but also of factual, works such as the scientific essay and the historical monograph. These accounts take three forms: (a) description by a writer of his own methods of working; (b) dialogue, usually in the form of correspondence, between a writer and a highly attuned respondent, such as a fellow writer or a gifted editor; and (c) analysis by professional critics or fellow writers of the evolution of a given piece of writing, from sources tapped to revision undertaken and completed. Second, there are dicta and directives about writing by authors and editors of rhetoric and composition texts and handbooks. Third, there is research dealing with the whole or some part of what has been called, globally, "the creative process"; or with a particular kind of creative behavior—the act of writing among adolescents.

These descriptions of the composing process present certain difficulties as sources of data. (1) The data are unsystematic: they do not deal with part or all of the composing process according to any shared set of strategies. (2) The statements provided by different sources of data contradict one another—more, they are often unique, even idiosyncratic. (3) Very few of the sources deal in adequate theoretical or empirical depth with how students of school age write. They answer very few of the following major and interesting questions about students as writers:

> If the context of student writing—that is, community milieu, school, family—affects the composing process, in what ways does it do so, and why?
>
> What are the resources students bring to the act of writing?
>
> If there are specifiable elements, moments, and stages in the composing process of students, what are these? If they can be differentiated, how? Can certain portions be usefully designated by traditional nomenclature, such as planning, writing, and revising? Are elements organized linearly in the writing process? recursively? in some other manner? How do these elements, moments, and stages in the composing process relate to one another?

If there is a phenomenon "prewriting," how can it be characterized?

What is a plan for a piece of writing? When and why do students have or not have a plan?

Under what conditions—physical, psychic—do students start to write?

If writing is essentially a selection among certain sorts of options— lexical, syntactic, rhetorical—what governs the choices students make?

What psychological factors affect or accompany portions of the writing process? What effects do they have? What is a block in writing (other than dysgraphia)? When and why do students have blocks? How can they be overcome?

Under what conditions do students stop work on a given piece of writing?

If all, or certain kinds of, writing within schools differs from all, or certain kinds of, writing outside schools, how do they differ and why?

If there are modes of school writing, how can these be differentiated? If the mode in which a piece is written affects the process of writing, or the process the mode, how?

What is the press of such variables as the reading of others' writing and the personal intervention of others upon any portion or upon the totality of the writing process?

Accounts by and about Established Writers

On the established writer as a useful source of data about writing, an investigator can say simply with the novelist Peter de Vries, "Don't ask the cow to analyze milk";[1] or he can examine this source.

If he does, he finds that writers' comments on how they write assume many modes. Occasionally, prose writers and poets write about their writing within their novels, short stories and poems: James Joyce in *Portrait of the Artist as a Young Man,* Thomas Mann in "Tonio Kröger," and Wordsworth in "The Prelude" are examples. In addition, they write about their own writing in diaries, journals, note-books, letters, prefaces to their own and to others' works, essays, full-length critical studies, autobiographical sketches and full-length self-studies, and interviews recorded in print, on record, and on film.[2]

As the range of modes chosen suggests, writers describe their methods of working and their attitudes toward writing for different reasons. With modes where the writer's audience is initially and per-haps ultimately himself—as in diaries, journals, and notebooks not written for publication, and in certain kinds of letters—the writer is usually concerned with working out a specific problem in the evolution of a specific piece of writing. These modes are expressive: they repre-sent a private forum where, to paraphrase E.M. Forster, a writer can discover how he thinks or feels about a matter by seeing what he has said. Self-discovery, compression or partiality of expression, immediacy, and uniqueness of stimulus characterize descriptions in these modes.

With modes such as the critical essay and the extended auto-biography, an audience other than oneself must be acknowledged. Consequently, amenities aiding an audience are observed: accounts are more formal in diction and in organization, and more elaborated. These accounts also tend to be retrospective affairs, and consequently reportorial in approach.

By their quite different natures, these two basic sets of modes present different kinds of difficulty as data. Descriptions in the ex-pressive mode are frankly idiosyncratic: they purport to be true only for an *N* of 1—a single writer who is pursuing, particularly if he is a major writer, a unique problem. Perhaps the most powerful con-temporary expression of the problem of uniqueness are these lines from "East Coker" by T.S. Eliot:

> So here I am, in the middle way, having had twenty years—
> Twenty years largely wasted, the years of *l'entre deux guerres*—
> Trying to learn to use words, and every attempt
> Is a wholly new start, and a different kind of failure
> Because one has only learnt to get the better of words
> . . . .
> . . .a new beginning, a raid on the inarticulate
> . . . .
> In the general mess of imprecision of feeling,
> Undisciplined squads of emotion.[3]

Descriptions in modes involving an audience other than oneself present other kinds of difficulties. Since these accounts are retro-spective, a possible difficulty with such data is the high probability of the inaccuracy of the account, incurred in part by the time-lag between the writing and the description of that writing.

A second, related difficulty is that not only are accounts *post hoc* affairs, most of those published are by writers who work almost ex-clusively in the imaginative modes and who have been rewarded by publisher and public for their fictive endeavors. One thinks of D.H. Lawrence's comment in *Studies in Classic American Literature* that all of the old American artists were hopeless liars: that only their art-speech was to be trusted as an accurate revelation of their thoughts and feelings; and he wonders if the observation may not justly be extended to imaginative writers of all nationalities and all eras when they talk about their methods of writing.[4]

In a recent interview the poet-critic John Ciardi speaks directly of this matter:

> N [Roy Newquist, the interviewer]: If you would, I'd like you to read a few of your poems and comment on them—how they happened to be written, perhaps, or what you were driving at.
>
> Ciardi: You're asking for lies. It's inevitable. I've been asked to do this over and over again, and lies come out.
>
> Let me put it this way. The least a poem can be is an act of skill. An act of skill is one in which you have to do more things at one time than you have time to think about. Riding a bike is an act of skill. If you stop to think of what you're doing at each of the balances, you'd fall off the bike. Then someone would come along and ask you to rationalize what you thought you were doing. Well, you write a poem. And somebody comes along and asks you to rationalize what you thought you were doing. You pick out a theme and you're hung with trying to be consistent with the theme you've chosen. You have to doubt every explanation.
>
> Nobody has worked harder than Valéry, the French poet, in trying to explain how he produced certain poems. He answers with every qualification in the world—touching this and that but ultimately lying. You have to end up lying. You know that you had something in your mind, but you can never get it straight.[5]

In addition to unintentional lies, some writers very openly admit they try to throw interviewer and public off the scent, usually because they fear any conscious, explicit probing into their methods of work will, to use Hemingway's verb, "spook" their writing. In the recorded interviews granted by such writers they are usually quite frank about their reluctance to discuss their actual methods of work.

Finally, both kinds of accounts share a difficulty: they focus upon the feelings of writers about the difficulties of writing—or not writing—almost to the exclusion of an examination of the act itself. A very wide survey of writers' accounts reveals this preoccupation: Nelson Algren, Arnold Bennett, Joseph Conrad, Simone de Beauvoir, Guy de Maupassant, F. Scott Fitzgerald, E.M. Forster, Andre Gide, John Keats, Norman Mailer, Katherine Mansfield, Jean Paul Sartre, Robert Louis Stevenson, Leo Tolstoi, Mark Van Doren, H.G. Wells, and Virginia Woolf are but some of the writers for whom this generalization holds true.[6]

Perhaps one of the best-known and dramatic examples of this preoccupation with writing difficulties is Virginia Woolf in A Writer's Diary. Although she makes occasional allusion to formal problems in her novels and even in the diary itself, she writes constantly about her feelings, usually negative, about the evolution of her works and about their critical reception by a coterie of friends-and-critics. She finds sustaining her energies after beginning her novels an especial source of difficulty. Here, for example, are excerpts describing her struggles with *Jacob's Room:*

> My mind turned by anxiety, or other cause, from its scrutiny of blank paper, is like a lost child—wandering the house, sitting on the bottom step to cry.
>
> (December 5, 1919)[7]

and

> It is worth mentioning, for future reference, that the creative power which bubbles so pleasantly in beginning a new book quiets down after a time, and one goes on more steadily. Doubts creep in. Then one becomes resigned. Determination not to give in, and the sense of an impending shape keep one at it more than anything. I'm a little anxious. How am I to bring off this conception? Directly one gets to work one is like a person walking, who has seen the country stretching out before. I want to write nothing in this book that I don't enjoy writing. Yet writing is always difficult.
>
> (May 29, 1923)[8]

The limitation in referring to these forms of data exclusively, then, is that they focus on partial phenomena. They often describe brilliantly the context, the affective milieu of the writing act; but the act itself remains undescribed.

Dialogue between Writer and Attuned Respondent

A second form of data about the composing process is the dialogue, usually in the form of correspondence about an imaginative work in progress, between a writer and a highly attuned respondent, such as a fellow artist or a skilled editor. In the first category, possibly one of the best-known technical correspondences is that between Gerard Manley Hopkins and Robert Bridges during the second half of the nineteenth century. Their letters, written over a period of twenty-four years from 1865 to 1889, often deal with formal problems each encountered in individual poems, with technical criticism of each other's poetry, and with their evolving theories of rhythm and versification.[9]

Understandably, correspondence between a writer and his editor, when not mercantile, is usually technical. In American letters perhaps the best-known correspondence in this category is that between the novelist Thomas Wolfe and Maxwell Perkins, his editor at Charles Scribner's publishing house.[10] A second, more recent example is the correspondence between the critic Malcolm Cowley and William Faulkner detailing the history of the Viking Portable Library edition of Faulkner's works.[11]

Inherently interesting as this form of data is, it, too, has limited value for a full inquiry into writing because it does not deal with the total process; rather, it focuses on only one part of the process, the revision specific to a given piece of work—for example, Hopkins' problems with "The Wreck of the Deutschland," or Wolfe's, with *Look Homeward, Angel*. Indeed, this specificity may be its major limitation in that the observations on these acts of revision may therefore be imperfectly generalizable.

Analyses by Others of Evolutions of Certain Pieces of Writing

Another form of data about writing is analysis of the evolution of a piece of writing by someone other than the author. Sometimes the analysts are fellow writers, as with Henry James's study of Hawthorne or John Berryman's of Stephen Crane. Sometimes the analysts are critics, as with Josephine Bennett's study, *The Evolution of "The Faerie Queene,"* and Butt and Tillotson's study, *Dickens at Work*.

These analysts focus upon different moments in the evolution of certain pieces. For some, focus is upon the early stages—sources read and recorded in notebooks and other accounts by the writer that later resonate in a work; for others, focus is upon the later stages—upon revisions, changes the writer makes in drafts that lead to, or even follow, initial publication.

Perhaps the best-known example of focus upon the early, upon what might even be called the prewriting, activities of the writer, is *The Road to Xanadu* by John Livingston Lowes, in which Lowes traces the sources through Coleridge's labyrinthine and cryptic notebook allusions to his reading for every aspect of "Kubla Khan" and "The Rime of the Ancient Mariner," from individual word choice to total thematic organization.

Although there is probably no one analysis of a prose work that holds the critical esteem of Lowes's analysis, a representative study is Jerome Beaty's *Middlemarch, From Notebook to Novel*. Focussing on chapter 81 as exemplar, Beaty juxtaposes his own direct analyses of Eliot's process of composing with accounts by her husband, John Cross; her publisher, John Blackwood; a biographer, Joan Bennett; and by the author herself. He finds a dissonance between his analyses and all other accounts which state or imply that Eliot wrote the scene between Dorothea and Rosamond in a "stroke of creative genius" with little prefiguring and less revision.*

Beaty's analyses of Eliot's notebook entries reveal that she planned for this chapter as she planned for other chapters in the novel:

> The plans for Chapter 81 are not particularly detailed—there was no attempt to sketch the stages of the conversation or the form of the dialogue—but then no chapter in *Middlemarch* was planned in that manner; it was not George Eliot's way. But it *was* planned for. All the motives and events, for example, are in the notebook that Dorothea has returned out of pity. That Rosamond is "wrought upon" by this pity of love, and that she tells Dorothea that it is Dorothea Will loves.[13]

His studies of the manuscript also reveal that not only was chapter 81 revised, "this chapter was more heavily revised than most of the others in *Middlemarch,* and revised in almost all its aspects: timing, content, point of view, characterization, tone, and outcome."[14]

Beaty concludes his analysis of chapter 81:

> Writing, to George Eliot, was not an unpremeditated outpouring; neither was it a mechanical following of detailed blueprint. It was a process of evolution and of discovery.[15]

Whatever the motivation behind George Eliot's statements, the discrepancies between her description and Beaty's findings also serve to make suspect yet another writer's account as a valid source of data about his own process of writing, while at the same time suggesting the value of direct analysis of writers' notebooks and drafts as sources of information about the writing process.

Other analysts have been interested instead in the process of revision or the transmutation of elements in original or early drafts into the burnished rightness of the final form. An early example in poetry criticism is M.R. Ridley's detailed examination of the drafts of certain poems by John Keats—specifically, "The Eve of St. Agnes" and the four major odes. More recent is *W.B. Yeats: The Later Poetry* by Thomas Parkinson, specifically chapter two, "Vestiges of Creation," and chapter four, "The Passionate Syntax." Studies of the revisions of prose works include Rudolf Arnheim's *Poets at Work* and an interesting casebook *Word for Word,* prepared by Wallace Hildick, in

---

* Beaty attributes the statements, at least by Cross and Eliot herself, to a shared belief in the Romantic notion of inspiration prevalent in the nineteenth century, even into the Victorian period:

"Their best work . . . was written without premeditation, in a frenzy of inspiration. Therefore it follows that revision and hard work are the signs of those who are less than geniuses."[12]

which are set forth for student examination "authors' alterations" by T.S. Eliot, D.H. Lawrence, Alexander Pope, Samuel Butler, Thomas Hardy, William Wordsworth, Henry James, William Blake, and Virginia Woolf.*

Literary critics have always studied style; in recent years scholars of style have made increasing use of linguistic analysis, often employing a computer. At times their cluster of techniques has been applied to works of disputed or shared authorship. Frederick Mosteller and David Wallace, for example, examined the Federalist Papers to ascertain whether John Jay or James Madison was the author of disputed passages, as well as what part Thomas Jefferson played in the revisions. In 1963, Bernard O'Donnell examined Stephen Crane's posthumously published novel, *The O'Ruddy*, to ascertain what parts of the work were actually written by Crane and what parts by the reporter who completed the novel.

Computer analysis of style has also been employed to make a comparative examination of grammatical and lexical elements in authors' styles. J.B. Carroll, for example, attempted by factor analysis to delineate "the basic dimensions on which style varied"; and he demonstrated that the style of Mickey Spillane and F. Scott Fitzgerald varied along certain specifiable dimensions. Boder showed that the verb-adjective quotient was a significant index of stylistic differences

---

* Certain themes emerge from a reading of these studies. One is the primacy of artifact over nature as stimulus to imaginative writing. What the writer has read seems more crucial than whatever is meant by direct confrontations with nature and other kinds of experience. This thesis has also been propounded for painters and other artists by Andre Malraux in *Les Voix du Silence*.

A second awareness is the validity of a distinction made by Stephen Spender in his essay "The Making of a Poem" between Mozartians and Beethovians. In her essay "The Uses of the Unconscious in Composing," this investigator elaborated Spender's distinctions:

The Morzartian is one who can instantaneously arrange encounters with his unconscious; he is one in whom the creative self leads a constant and uninterrupted life of its own, serene to surface disturbances, oblivious of full upper activity—coach-riding, concert-giving, bill-paying. The Mozartian can "plunge the greatest depths of his own experience by the tremendous effort of a moment" and surface every time with a finished pearl—a Cosi Fan Tutte, a Piano Concerto in C Major.

The Beethovian, on the other hand, is the agonizer, the evolutionizer. Scholars studying his first notes to a quartet or a symphony, as Spender points out, are astounded by their embryonic clumsiness. The creative self in a Beethovian is not a plummeting diver, but a plodding miner who seems at times to scoop south with his bare bands. To change the metaphor, for the Beethovian, composing is not unlike eating an artichoke—pricks and inadequate rewards in our tedious leaf-by-leaf spiraling toward the delectable heart.[16]

among professional and student writers. There are certain general computer programs for handling language data, such as Iker and Harway's work with content analysis, and Stone and Boles's *General Inquirer Program*.

Although in these linguistic studies the process of writing is sometimes purportedly under scrutiny, to this writer's knowledge none of the investigators has yet attempted to develop generalizations from their studies of specific works and authors. They have not attempted, in other words, to delineate *the,* even *a,* writing process or to ascertain whether the process has constant characteristics across writers. Rather, they have been concerned with product- rather than process-centered research.

Rhetoric and Composition Texts and Handbooks

Another possible source of data about the composing process is the rhetoric or composition text which gives students dicta and directives about how to speak and write. The best-known classical rhetorics are of course Plato, Aristotle, Cicero, and Quintilian. These have provided the models for theory, and applications, down the centuries. Contemporary examples of rhetoric texts include Francis X. Connolly's *A Rhetoric Casebook,* Leo Rockas's *Models of Rhetoric,* and Martin, Ohmann and Wheatley's *The Logic and Rhetoric of Exposition.*

Composition handbooks—a more recent development—also give dicta and directives; but, unlike most of the rhetoric texts, they cite no substantiation for them. (See, for example, Warriner's handbook). The authors and editors of these texts neither state nor imply that they have tapped any of the following possible sources of data, if not substantiation: (a) introspection into their own processes of writing; (b) accounts by and about professional writers; and (c) accounts of and about secondary students, the audience to whom their advice is purportedly directed.

In America, beginning probably with John Walker's *A Teacher's Assistant in English Composition* (1803), composition texts served a different audience from that of rhetoric texts: whereas the rhetoric text was designed to help prepare young men of the upper classes for the pulpit, bar, and public forum, the composition text was designed to help younger students of both sexes in the middle and lower classes achieve a basic written literacy. In his survey of the rhetorical tradition Edward P.J. Corbett notes these differences in the two approaches to teaching writing:

Rhetoric courses in the schools gradually assumed a new orientation—the study of the four forms of discourse: exposition, argumentation, description, and narration. The virtues that were stressed in this approach to composition were unity, coherence, and emphasis. Style continued to engage some attention, but the focus shifted from the schemes and tropes to a concern for diction (which gradually deteriorated into a neurotic concern for "correct usage") and for syntax (which, under the popular handbooks, became a rather negative approach to "correct grammar"). The study of the paragraph concentrated on the topic sentence and the various ways of developing the topic sentence to achieve maximum unity, coherence, and emphasis.[17]

The characterization these texts convey of the composing process is of a quite conscious, wholly rational—at times, even mechanical—affair with many of the components for a piece of discourse extrinsic to the speaker or writer. For example, *inventio,* the first *division* of classical rhetoric, does not refer to the writer's finding within his own experience the sources of his discourse; it refers rather to discovering, in the universe outside, the *topoi,* or "the set of sources available . . . in my argument."[18] The organization of a piece of writing, particularly a speech, is, if one believes Cicero and others, fixed by a traditional schema consisting of six parts: exordium, narrative, partition, confirmation, repetition, peroration. A speaker or writer does not evolve a mode of organization that is indigenous to a specific content: he follows instead the six-part outline.

How the writer feels about the subject matter and how his feelings may influence what he writes—the affective dimension—are not really considered in these texts. The notion that there might be a press of personality upon all components of the process is not present. This is not a criticism of the classical texts; it is an historical comment. The rhetorical tradition is simply, in its major works, significantly prior to the development of psychology with its interests in introspection and theories of personality development. Because they do not consider the possible effect of a writer's personality upon the process, however, rhetoric and composition texts are not a useful source of data for most of the questions posed earlier in this chapter.

Theory of the Creative Process

Research is a third source of data that might provide a theoretical base or a methodological model for this inquiry. The two modes examined in this section are (1) theoretical studies of what is called, globally, "the creative process," and (2) pieces of empirical research dealing with the writing of adolescents.

In *The Art of Thought* (1926) Graham Wallas typologizes creative thought as a four-stage process—a delineation that persists, with occasional shifts and changes of terms and categories, into the present literature. Wallas credits Helmholtz, the German physicist, with first describing three stages in the process; the fourth Wallas adds along with descriptive terms for all four stages:

> We can . . . roughly dissect out a continuous process, with a beginning and a middle and an end of its own. . . . Helmholtz, . . . speaking in 1891 at a banquet on his seventieth birthday, described the way in which his most important new thoughts had come to him. He said that after previous investigation of the problem "in all directions . . . happy ideas come unexpectedly without effort, like an inspiration. So far as I am concerned, they have never come to me when my mind was fatigued, or when I was at my working table. . . . They came particularly readily during the slow ascent of wooded hills on a sunny day." Helmholtz here gives us three stages in the formation of a new thought. The first in time I shall call Preparation, the stage during which the problem was 'investigated . . . in all directions'; the second is the stage during which he was not consciously thinking about the problem, which I shall call Incubation; the third, consisting of the appearance of the 'happy idea' together with the psychological events which immediately preceded and accompanied that appearance, I shall call Illumination.
>
> And I shall add a fourth stage, of Verification, which Helmholtz does not here mention . . . in which both the validity of the idea was tested, and the idea itself was reduced to exact form.[19]

Many students of creativity as well as creators across modes—painting, composing—share this view of the creative process. Writing, for example, which can be regarded as a species of creative behavior, is often described in quite similar terms. In his introduction to *Writers at Work: The Paris Review Interviews*, Malcolm Cowley describes the composing process shared by the short-story writers and novelists interviewed:

> There would seem to be four stages in the composition of a story. First comes the germ of the story, then the period of more or less conscious meditation, then the first draft, and finally the revision, which may be simply "pencil work," as John O'Hara calls it—that is, minor changes in wording—or may lead to writing several drafts and what amounts to a new work.[20]

In the process of writing, revision seems to occupy the same place that verification holds in scientific and mathematical inquiries.

Another view of the specific poetic process as a sequence of *five* (perhaps six) aligned stages is presented by the psychologist R.N. Wilson in his essay "Poetic Creativity, Process and Personality":

A rough paradigm of the stages of poetic creativity would include at least the following elements: the selective perception of the environment; the acquisition of technique; the envisioning of combinations and distillations; elucidation of the vision; and the end of the poem and its meaning to the poet.[21]

This sequence differs from Wallas's chiefly in regarding the acquisition of technique as an element in the process (it is probable the acquisition of technique is regarded instead as a requisite *to* the process by Wallas and others); and in its concern with the end of the process, a later element than "elucidation" which for Wilson includes revision, Wallas's fourth stage, and the contemplation of the product.

In the literature there are perhaps only two markedly different characterizations of creation as something other than a process of several aligned stages. One characterization represents it as the tension generated between a single or multiple set of opposing variables; the second, as the point or moment of intersection between two disparate modes or fields of endeavor.

The earliest description of creation as the tension generated between a single set of polarities is probably Plato's dialogue *Ion*, with the movement of the artist between frenzy (divine inspiration) and formulation. The best-known is perhaps Freud's interpretation of creativity, in "The Relation of the Poet to Day-Dreaming" (1908) and "Leonardo da Vinci and a Memory of His Childhood" (1910), as the tension between the unconscious and conscious activities of the mind. In *Neurotic Distortion of the Creative Process*, L. S. Kubie also dichotomizes the activities of the mind during creation; but he suggests that creative behaviors emanate from the preconscious rather than the unconscious portion of the mind. Kubie describes the distinctive features of preconscious processes as

their automatic and subtle recordings of multiple perceptions, their automatic recall, their multiple analogic and overlapping linkages, and their direct connections to the autonomic processes which underlie affective states.[22]

In his essay "The Conditions of Creativity" (1962), Jerome Bruner describes creation as the tension produced among a multiple set of "antimonies."[23] These are detachment and commitment, passion and decorum, freedom from and domination by the artifact, deferral and immediacy, and conflicting identities within the creator. Creators are at once "disengaged from that which exists conventionally" and "engaged deeply in what they construct to replace it"; urgently vital in artistic impulse and courteous and formal in artistic expression;

separated from the object and bored enough by creating it to put off completion until the psychologically appropriate time; and involved through their creation in "working out of conflict and coalition within the set of identities that compose" their personality.[24]

Another markedly different characterization of creativity is proffered by Arthur Koestler in his massive study, *The Act of Creation* (1964). Koestler describes creation, not as the outcome of a series of aligned stages nor as the result of tension between "antimonies," but rather as the intersection of two disparate "matrices." "Matrix" he defines as "any ability, habit, or skill, any pattern of ordered behavior governed by a 'code' of fixed rules."[25] In Koestler's view, creation is "bisociative"; that is, the creator perceives "a situation or event in two habitually incompatible associative contexts."[26] Humor, literary creation, and scientific discovery are examples Koestler gives of bisociative activity.

Viewed singly, these three delineations of creation may seem descriptions of fact. Juxtaposed, however, they reveal their hypothetical nature. That there are data supporting all three sets of hypotheses suggests there may be process*es* of creation with quite different profiles or typographies. Indeed, there is the strong possibility that other delineations are equally valid.

Empirical Research about Adolescent Writing

Most pieces of empirical research on the adolescent writer focus upon the product(s) rather than upon the process(es) of their writing and, consequently, do not provide an appropriate methodology for a process-centered inquiry. Of the 504 studies written before 1963 that are cited in the bibliography of *Research in Written Composition,* only two deal even indirectly with the process of writing among adolescents.*

---

* These are the unpublished dissertations, "Proposals for the Conduct of Written Composition Activities in the Secondary School Inherent in an Analysis of the Language Composition Act" by Lester Angene and "Factors Affecting Regularity of the Flow of Words during Written Composition" by John A. Van Bruggen. Angene looks only at finished student themes: any examples and statements involving the process of writing he draws from a sample of professional writers and from analysis of the writing act in one composition handbook, written by his advisor. Van Bruggen's emphasis, as the title of his study makes clear, is the physical rate at which a sample of eighty-four junior high school students write— more specifically, how often and how fast they actually place pen to paper (actually stylus to electric disc) in the production of their themes. The process of writing, beyond this series of physical contacts between pen and paper, remains unexamined.

Two recent American studies which focus upon process rather than upon product of composition are "The Sound of Writing" by Anthony Tovatt and Ebert L. Miller and *Pre-Writing: The Construction and Application of Models for Concept Formation in Writing* by D. Gordon Rohman and Albert O. Wiecke.

Tovatt's study proceeds from the premise that "we write with our ears" and that if students can "hear" what they are writing, they can transmute satisfactory patterns of written discourse. In the first experimental year of the study (1964-65) thirty ninth-grade students, matched with a control class, were given the OAV (oral-aural-visual) stimuli approach to writing. As one of the two most significant—or at least unique—features of the experiment, the students used tape-recorders equipped with audio-active headsets so that they could hear themselves electronically as they composed. A second was that the teacher provided a constant role-model as writer by composing in the presence of the experimental class until they "eventually accept[ed] the fact good writing is achieved through sustained labor in three basic stages: prewriting, writing, and rewriting."[27]

Tovatt reports these findings:

> The OAV stimuli procedures demonstrated in the first year a general superiority over a conventional approach in increasing student abilities in writing, reading, listening, and language usage. However, rating of compositions from the control and experimental classes was inconclusive in establishing the superiority of either approach.[28]

In the study by Rohman and Wiecke, the investigators divide the writing process into three stages: "prewriting," "writing," and "rewriting." They focus upon prewriting—which they define as "the stage of discovery in process when a person assimilates 'his subject' to himself"—because prewriting "is crucial to the success of any writing that occurs later" and "is seldom given the attention it consequently deserves."[29]

In a project involving three sections of a sophomore-level course in expository writing at Michigan State University in 1964, the investigators sought "(1) to isolate and describe the principle of this assimilation and (2) to devise a course that would allow students to imitate its dynamics."[30]

The principle of the assimilation, they decided, is the conversion of an "event" into an "experience," to use the words of novelist Dorothy S. Sayers. The three means they employed were (1) the keeping of a journal, (2) the practice of some principles derived from the religious meditation, and (3) the use of the analogy. The essays produced after a one-semester course with the emphasis on assimilation "showed a statistically significant superiority [one set, at the .05 level; one set, at the .01 level] to essays produced in control sections."[31]

Both the Tovatt-Miller and the Rohman-Wiecke studies are experiments in instruction: that is, systematic group interventions are introduced to effect a change in students' behavior as they write. The purpose of the present inquiry, on the other hand, is to attempt to describe how student writers usually or typically behave as they write with minimal direct intervention by the investigator. In other words, the Tovatt-Miller and the Rohman-Wiecke studies are efforts to instruct or teach; this inquiry is an effort to describe. Nevertheless, as two of the few serious efforts extant to examine writing in process for adolescent writers, they deserve acknowledgment and explication.

Conflicting Data

Among these three major sources of data there is often disagreement. Writers' accounts and composition texts, for example, present a powerful instance of the phenomenon noted at the beginning of this chapter—one set of sources that contradict or are often directly contradicted by another. Here, for example, are two accounts of how the writing process proceeds:

(1) A good writer puts words together in correct, smooth sentences, according to the rules of standard usage. He puts sentences together to make paragraphs that are clear and effective, unified and well developed. Finally, he puts paragraphs together into larger forms of writing—essays, letters, stories, research papers.

In practice, as you know from your own experience, a writer begins with a general plan and ends with details of wording, sentence structure, and grammar. First, he chooses the *subject* of his composition. Second, he tackles the *preparation* of his material, from rough ideas to final outline. Third, he undertakes the writing itself, once again beginning with a rough form (the first draft) and ending with a finished form (the final draft) that is as nearly perfect as he can make it.

These three basic stages of composition are almost always the same for any form of writing. Each of the three stages proceeds according to certain definite steps, listed below in order.

a. Choosing and limiting the subject	1. Subject
b. Assembling materials	
c. Organizing materials	2. Preparation
d. Outlining	
e. Writing the first draft	3. Writing
f. Revising	
g. Writing the final draft[32]	

(2) You will write . . . if you will write without thinking of the result in terms of a result, but think of the writing in terms of discovery, which is to say the creation must take place between the pen and the paper, not before in a thought, or afterwards in a recasting. Yes, before in a thought, but not in careful thinking. It will come if it is there and if you will let it come, and if you have anything you will get a sudden creative recognition. You won't know how it was, even what it is, but it will be creation if it came out of the pen and out of you and not out of an architectural drawing of the thing you are doing . . . I can tell how important it is to have that creative recognition. You cannot go into the womb to form the child; it is there and makes itself and comes forth whole—and there it is and you have made it and felt it, but it has come itself—and that is creative recognition. Of course you have a little more control over your writing than that; you have to know what you want to get; but when you know that, let it take you and if it seems to take you off the track don't hold back, because that is perhaps where instinctively you want to be and if you hold back and try to be always where you have been before, you will go dry.[33]

The first of these comes from Warriner's *English Grammar and Composition*, 11, one volume of a very widely used series of composition handbooks. The second is by the writer Gertrude Stein. Clearly, the statements are almost antithetical: according to Stein, writing is an act of discovery emanating "out of the pen and out of you" while Warriner's suggests writing is a tidy, accretive affair that proceeds by elaborating a fully pre-conceived and formulated plan.

Statements in composition texts and handbooks also differ from those of established writers in discussion of what might be called specific components in the writing process. Take this same matter of planning, for example. The quotation above from Warriner's handbook unequivocally states that a writer always makes an outline before "writing," regardless of the mode of writing.

In 1964 this investigator collected data from professional writers regarding their planning practices. Responding to a questionnaire about their planning practices were the following professional and academic writers: Max Bluestone, Reuben Brower, Jerome Bruner, John B. Carroll, John Ciardi, Kenneth Lynn, Raven I. McDavid, Harold Martin, Theodore Morrison, Henry Olds, James K. Robinson, Israel Scheffler, Clifford Shipton, B.F. Skinner, Priscilla Tyler, and Mark Van Doren.[34]

The data from these questionnaires belie the textbook generalization that all writers make written outlines for all forms of writing they do. Indeed, the data suggest there is great diversity and individuality in planning practices, at least among this sample of writers.

In the sample four of the sixteen writers—J.B. Carroll, James K. Robinson, Israel Scheffler, and B.F. Skinner—proceed as the texts state all writers do. That is, they make a rough outline, then an elaborated one complete with full sentences, indentations, and numbering and lettering of items. For these writers the outline seems to represent the major act in the writing process, as B.F. Skinner makes clear:

> When I begin to think of a developed paper or a book, I turn almost immediately to outlines. These grow in detail, almost to the point of producing the final prose.

And James K. Robinson notes the usefulness of the elaborated outline not only for himself but also for his students:

> I found both for myself and for students whom I have had in Freshman English that the sentence outline is most satisfactory since it forces one to make definite statements that will enable one to test logical relationships or developments in the paper to be written. It goes a step beyond words or phrases in planning.

Israel Scheffler also produces an outline that structures, as well as fully pre-figures, the final piece of writing:

> . . . The outline is as detailed as I can make it, with different systems of numbering and lettering, plus indentation, to reveal subordination and other relationships among the items. The main items I try to spell out as full sentences or short paragraphs, the subordinate items as sentences, clauses, or simply tags to indicate examples or other points. I worry about parallelism of items with parallel position in the outline, as well as subordination of other items.
>
> Normally, the outline does not cover all the details of the eventual draft, but I do want it to give the main structure of the whole in as explicit form as I can get it at the beginning.

The majority in the group take what might be called a middle position toward planning—that is, they make some kind of informal outline adapted to their individual styles of working and to the mode of the piece involved. Kenneth Lynn jots down in phrase form a sequence of items he plans to use, observing some system of identation. Harold Martin sets down phrases without any particular order, then groups these "for meaningful relationships," and finally marks "1-2-3 for order": he finds no value to "IA, la." Theodore Morrison calls the plan he makes for his novels "a quick conspectus": he uses "heads as a reminder of where I am going."

Members of this middle group seem to be against any plan that totally pre-figures a piece of writing. Their shared reason is aptly set forth by Max Bluestone:

The rough scheme [his form of plan] is a map to the territory of my thoughts. The map is never precise, first because the territory has not been thoroughly explored and second because writing is in itself the discovery of new territory. I usually anticipate discovery in the act of composition.

Contradicting another statement in Warriner's, writers in the sample who work in more than one mode proceed differently in different genres. Poetry seems to be a genre for which no outlines or elaborated plans are ever made, at least by the writers of poetry in this sample—Max Bluestone, John Ciardi, and Mark Van Doren.

Max Bluestone, Theodore Morrison, and Mark Van Doren, novelists and short story writers in the sample, also note for these modes they seldom make elaborate written outlines. They would seem to agree with the novelist Eileen Bassing about the use of the outline in fiction.

> N [Roy Newquist]: Could you outline your working procedures? Perhaps it's best to refer directly—if only roughly—to the production of *Home before Dark* and *Where's Annie?*
>
> *Bassing:* I'm glad you said "roughly" because I don't think I could give you a precise outline of any particular thing I write. I very much admire writers who can work from a neat, orderly outline, and I always feel that my method can only be called "chaotic." The complete outline isn't for me.
>
> I do have a shadowy outline in my mind—as I did in *Home before Dark,* for example. I knew what I wanted to say, and I knew a great deal about my central character. Once you have the chracter you're pretty well started, . . .
>
> . . . The outline, again [with her novel *Where's Annie?*] was very shadowy—I had the beginning, a kind of middle, a scene here and there, and maybe the end. . . .
>
> *N:* In other words you don't really work from an outline at the beginning. You work from an idea, or some characters, and write a first draft—then make an outline and write it again. Is that right?
>
> *Bassing:* Yes.
>
> *N:* Isn't that a very unusual way of working?
>
> *Bassing:* Is it? I don't think so.[35]

The single mode of exposition then is the only mode cited by this sample for which outlines are produced with any degree of regularity, and then only by *some* of these writers.

The data from the questionnaire also suggest that a second generalization of rhetoric texts and manuals about planning is not valid, at least for this sample of writers—that is, all planning precedes all writing as all writing precedes all revising. The metaphor implied in these accounts about the writing process is linear: each "stage" is monolithic and holds a fixed position in a lock-step chronological process. There are, in other words, no major recursive features in the writing process.

All writers in the sample state they do engage in some form of planning prior to the production of a piece of sustained discourse: for Reuben Brower and Jerome Bruner this takes the form of conversation with friends. They also state or imply, however, that they continue to plan and to adapt and revise previously written plans as the piece evolves. Theodore Morrison makes a conspectus "at such times as seem necessary or seem to offer help." Some of the writers even make written plans or outlines as part of their revising. Max Bluestone states that if he is revising "something that has lain fallow," he might make a revised outline as well, one that "usually has to do with compression and elaboration of the version before me." Clearly, for these authors the so-called "stages" of writing are not fixed in an inexorable sequence. Rather, they occur and reoccur throughout the process. These data then make suspect the straight line which rhetoric texts imply as an appropriate metaphor for the writing process.*

This discrepancy then between these two forms of data—the statements made about writing in composition texts and handbooks and statements by professional writers—make suspect the validity of one form, if not both forms, of data.

Another dissonance occurs between the statements made about the practice and value of outlining in composition texts, manuals, and textbooks and the actual practices of able secondary students as examined by empirical research. Modern rhetoric and composition texts, as the quotation above from Warriner's handbook suggests, present the formal outline as a customary prelude to student writing, at least in the mode of exposition.

In a pilot study conducted in 1964, this investigator examined two assumptions behind the generalization on outlining presented in Warriner's handbook. The first assumption is descriptive: student writers do organize by outlining. The second is normative: to assure the most

---

* An aside: there is almost perfect unanimity among authors in the sample that whatever training in formal outlining they received in school has no influence on their current planning practices. Mark Van Doren and Jerome Bruner put it mildly: "Formal training seemed artificial and didn't interest me."

Others react more strongly: "Such procedures have helped me not at all." (Kenneth Lynn) "It was forced upon me and I did what I had to do, but I resist such outlining as a destruction. It seems to imply that one may complete his thought process in the outline and then merely go for 'style' in the writing. Nonsense. The writing and the thinking are inseperable [sic]. Any other assumption can only produce hack-work." (John Ciardi).

skillfully organized theme, student writers should organize by formal outlining. These assumptions were treated as hypotheses and examined in the following ways.

If assumption one is true, if student writers do organize by outlining, it seemed logical to believe that superior student writers would use outlining in organizing a group of expository themes whether they were directed to or not. The only data that would yield such information were the total written evolutions of a number of student themes, from first recorded act through final submitted draft. To acquire such data, the investigator asked an eleventh-grade high honors English class of twenty-five students to save and to submit, with the final drafts of all expository themes written during an eight-week period, all written actions they performed in the course of writing these themes.

The students were given no directives about how these themes were to be organized. When one student asked, during the explanation about saving all materials, if the investigator expected to find outlines with every theme, the investigator said she had no set expectations about what she would find; she wanted only to have everything produced in the course of writing them, whatever these materials happened to be.

During the eight-week period the students submitted (as part or all

Table 1

Types of Outlines Accompanying 109 Expository Themes Written
By 25 Eleventh Grade Students

Theme Assignment	Total Number of Expository Themes Written	Total Number of Outlines	Number of Informal Outlines	Number of Formal Outlines
1.	25	15	9	6
2.	14	6	6	0
3.	23	6	5	1
4.	22	4	3	1
5.	25	9	8	1
Total	109	40	31	9

of five writing assignments) 109 expository themes together with all written actions that preceded the final drafts. Of these, 40 themes (or 36.7 percent) were accompanied by a plan, defined here as any schema related to the composition of the theme, prior to that theme. Of these plans, nine (or 8.3 percent) qualified as formal outlines by what are, conventionally, the minimal criteria for formality: numbers or letters precede the items, and there is at least one level of indentation. The remaining 91.7 percent were atypical according to the generalization set forth in Warriner's handbook. To conclude from these very scant data that the students from whom these themes were collected typically or customarily do not outline formally for more than eight percent of the themes they write, much more that *all* secondary students do not, is, of course, unwarranted. These data however shed additional doubt upon the validity of the generalization in the rhetoric and composition texts.

The second assumption in the teaching of the outline, that the writing of a formal outline assures a more successfully organized theme, was examined in the following way: perhaps the most common means of determining the success of organization of a theme is by teacher evaluation, specifically, by the grade given the theme. If the writing of an outline prior to the writing of the theme assures superior organization, it would seem to follow that the student theme which had been preceded by an outline would rank higher by teacher evaluation than the theme which had not.

To test this hypothesis, three independent judges who were experienced teachers of English were asked to grade, from the total of 109 themes submitted, a sample of 20; 9 of which had been accompanied by outlines—4 formal, 5 informal—and 11 of which had not. The judges were not told to what category any theme belonged. They were asked to evaluate each theme solely on the basis of its organization.*

After the three judges evaluated all 20 themes and submitted their grades, the grades were coded according to whether that theme was accompanied by a formal outline, by an informal outline, or by no outline at all. These data, analyzed by a program of covariant analysis, revealed no correlation between the presence or absence of any outline and the grade a student receives evaluating how well organized that theme is.

Conclusion

Some of the data presented in this chapter contribute either useful

---

* To assure that the judges would be evaluating what constituted good organization according to the same set of criteria, the investigator asked them to draw up a list on which they all agreed and on which they would base their grades. What constituted to each of them an A, B, and C was also informally discussed, and the judges agreed that an A should represent fulfillment of all criteria; B most of them; and C, some.

methodological or theoretical models for this inquiry.

The technique of the interview found in the accounts of professional writers is scarcely unique to this form of data; but as one helpful means for eliciting information from student writers, it will also be employed in this inquiry. The provocative and rich responses to certain kinds of questions, especially those posed in the *Paris Review* interviews, recommend such questions as those on prewriting be asked in this study as well.

Although, as the brief review of rhetoric and composition texts revealed, these data do not provide generative category-systems, several of the theories of creativity do. Examples include the attenuation of the poetic or creative process suggested by R.N. Wilson, particularly the notions that the "selective perception of the environment" and the contemplation of a product and its "meaning" represent components to describe if they apply to the composing process of students. The four-stage description of the process delineated by Helmholtz, Wallas, and Cowley will serve as the center of the delineation of the writing process in this study.

CHAPTER 2

THE DESIGN OF THE STUDY

Eight sixteen- and seventeen-year-old secondary school students serve as subjects for the following case studies: five girls and three boys.* Six are white; one, black; one, Chinese-American. They come from various types of secondary schools in the greater metropolitan area of Chicago: (1) an all-white upper-middle-class suburban high school; (2) a racially and economically mixed high school in a small city north of Chicago, often named among the ten best high schools in the United States; (3) a racially mixed and lower-middle-class suburban high school in an industrial area west of the city; (4) a racially and economically mixed comprehensive Chicago high school; (5) an almost all-black ghetto school in Chicago; and (6) a private, university-affiliated laboratory school.

The investigator had access to the school records of five of the subjects; the records indicate that of these five, three have above-average intelligence and two, average. The remaining three subjects, for whom the investigator did not have access to school records, reported having scored 670 or higher on both the verbal and quantitative sections of College Entrance Board Examinations, suggesting that they should be considered to have above-average intelligence.

Six of the subjects are characterized by the chairman of the English departments at their high schools, who recommended their selection, as "good" writers; and three of the eight (two girls and a boy) were selected as NCTE Achievement Awards winners for their schools.† The other two are characterized by their most recent teachers of English as interested in writing but not particularly able as writers.

Each subject met four times with the investigator. At the first session, following an informal conversation of approximately twenty minutes,

---

* More girls than boys volunteered to participate and, once in the study, stayed until all data were collected.

† These awards, which are given annually on a proportionate basis across the fifty states, were based on judges' assessments of the student's autobiography, an impromptu theme, supporting comments from his current teacher of English, and his scores on two standardized tests: one in writing and one in literary awareness.

the subject, in the presence of the investigator, simultaneously composed aloud and wrote down a short piece in whatever mode and of whatever subject matter he wished. The composing aloud was recorded by a tape recorder. In addition, the subject, in this and subsequent sessions, sat in a position where it was possible for the investigator to observe and make notes on his actions.

At the end of the first session, the subject was given the stimulus, "Write about a person, event, or idea that particularly intrigues you," and asked to write his responses at the second session a week hence. In addition, the subject was asked to bring any written prefigurings he had made for this piece of writing.

At the second session the subject again composed aloud. Also, he was asked to recall whatever prewriting and planning he did in the period between sessions; and these recollections, with expansions and elucidations gained by investigator questioning, were also recorded.

At the end of the second session, the subject was told that at the third session, which would occur approximately a week later, he would be asked to recall as completely as possible all the writing he had ever done, both inside and outside school. The investigator recommended consultations with parents and former teachers, if available. Also, she requested the subject bring in whatever samples of his writing, produced at any age, were still in his or others' possession.

At the third session each subject gave a writing autobiography that included related reading experiences and descriptions and evaluations of the teaching of writing he had experienced. All but two subjects brought samples of past writing—including, in one case, two pieces written when the subject was four.

At the end of this session, the investigator asked that the subject bring with him to the fourth session a piece of imaginative writing—a story, poem, sketch, or personal narrative—which he was to write during the intervening week or ten days. (It should be noted here that, with one exception, all data were collected during a summer vacation; and even though subjects were involved with summer school or summer jobs, they had more time available for writing than during the regular school year.) The subject was asked to bring any plans and drafts associated with this piece. At this session, in addition to recalling his prewriting and possible planning, the subject recounted the total process he engaged in while writing the piece. This account, like the others, was tape recorded, and transcripts were subsequently made from the tapes.

The purpose of the three stimuli provided was to assure that the subject produced writing in the two major modes, reflexive and extensive. In practice, however, these stimuli did not work out as planned. Although directions given the subject concerning the first piece of writing encouraged personal reflexive writing, every subject produced for the first session a piece in the extensive mode—a choice that might be regarded as some kind of comment upon the mode with which the subject was most comfortable and easy and/or the one which he had been asked more regularly to produce in school. In the second session, the investigator again attempted, through the assigned stimulus, to elicit a piece of writing in the reflexive mode. The responses, however, with one exception, were not engaged, nor even very personalized.

The purpose of the fourth session was to secure a description of the writing process connected with the writing of a piece of poetry or fiction. Six of the eight responded to this assignment: all five of the girls in the sample and only one of the three boys. Of the other two boys, one wrote what he characterized as a "piece of obscenity"; and the second refused to write any response at all.

CHAPTER 3

THE COMPOSING PROCESS: MODE OF ANALYSIS

The purpose of this chapter is to delineate dimensions of the composing process among secondary school students, against which case studies of twelfth-grade writers can be analyzed. As with some of the accounts of the creative process in chapter 1, the premise of this chapter is that there are elements, moments, and stages within the composing process which can be distinguished and characterized in some detail.

This delineation is presented in two forms: as an outline (see pp. 34-35) and as a narrative. The use of an outline, which is of course linear and single layered, to describe a process, which is laminated and recursive, may seem a paradoxical procedure; but its purpose is to give a category system against which the eight case studies can be examined. The narrative portion, in contrast, is an attempt to convey the actual density and "blendedness" of the process.

Although this category system is set forth before the analysis of the data, it was derived from an extensive analysis of the eight case studies. The procedure for analyzing the data was inductive; the presentation is deductive.

Dimensions of the Composing Process among Twelfth-Grade Writers: A Narrative

The first dimension of the composing process to note is the *nature of the stimulus* that activates the process or keeps it going. For students, as for any other writers, stimuli are either self encountered or other initiated. Either the student writes from stimuli with which he has privately interacted or from stimuli presented by others—the most common species of the second being, of course, the assignment given by the teacher. Both kinds of stimuli can be nonverbal or verbal, although it is an extremely rare and sophisticated teacher who can give a nonverbal writing assignment.

All areas of experience, or fields of discourse, can provide the stimuli for writing. It is useful to pause here to present the schema of regis-

Dimensions of the Composing Process among Twelfth-Grade Writers:
An Outline

1. Context of Composing
Community, Family, School

2. Nature of Stimulus
Registers:

Field of Discourse—encounter with natural environment; encounter with induced environment or artifacts; human relationships; self.

Mode of Discourse—expressive-reflexive; expressive-extensive.

Tenor of Discourse

Self-Encountered Stimulus

Other-Initiated Stimulus:

Assignment by Teacher—external features (student's relation to teacher; relation to peers in classroom; relation to general curriculum and to syllabus in English; relation to other work in composition); internal features or specification of assignment (registers, linguistic formulation, length, purpose, audience, deadline, amenities, treatment of written outcome, other).

Reception of Assignment by Student—nature of task, comprehension of task, ability to enact task, motivation to enact task.

3. Prewriting
Self-Sponsored Writing:

Length of Period

Nature of Musings and Elements Contemplated—field of discourse; mode of written discourse; tenor or formulating of discourse.

Interveners and Interventions—self, adults (parent, teacher, other), peers (sibling, classmate, friend); type of intervention (verbal, nonverbal), time of intervention, reason for intervention (inferred), effect of intervention on writing, if any.

Teacher-Initiated (or School-Sponsored) Writing:

(Same categories as above)

4. Planning
Self-Sponsored Writing:

Initial Planning—length of planning; mode of planning (oral; written: jottings, informal list of words/phrases, topic outline, sentence outline); scope; interveners and interventions.

Later Planning—length of planning; mode; scope; time of occurrence; reason; interveners and interventions.

Teacher-Initiated Writing:
(Same categories as above)

5. Starting
Self-Sponsored Writing:

Seeming Ease or Difficulty of Decision

Element Treated First Discursively—seeming reason for initial selection of that element; eventual placement in completed piece.

Context and Conditions under Which Writing Began

Interveners and Interventions

Teacher-Initiated Writing:
(Same categories as above)

6. Composing Aloud: A Characterization

Selecting and Ordering Components:

Anticipation / Abeyance — what components projected; when first noted orally; when used in written piece.

Kinds of Transformational Operations—addition (right-branching, left-branching); deletion; reordering or substitution; embedding.

Style—preferred transformations, if any; "program" of style behind preferred transformations (source: self, teacher, parent, established writer, peer); (effect on handling of other components—lexical, rhetorical, imagaic).

Other Observed Behaviors:

Silence—physical writing; silent reading; "unfilled" pauses.

Vocalized Hesitation Phenomena—filler sounds (selected phonemes; morphemes of semantically-low content; phrases and clauses of semantically-low content); critical comments (lexis; syntax; rhetoric); expressions of feelings and attitudes (statements, expressions of emotion—pleasure/pain) toward self as writer to reader; digressions (ego-enhancing; discourse-related).

Tempo of Composing:

Combinations of Composing and Hesitational Behaviors

Relevance of Certain Theoretical Statements concerning Spontaneous Speech

7. Reformulation

Type of Task:

Correcting; Revising; Rewriting

Transforming Operations:

Addition—kind of element;

stated or inferred reason for addition.

Deletion—kind of element; stated or inferred reason for deletion.

Reordering or Substitution—kind of element; stated or inferred reason.

Embedding—kind of element; stated or inferred reason.

8. Stopping

Formulation:

Seeming Ease or Difficulty of Decision

Element Treated Last—seeming reason for treating last; placement of that element in piece.

Context and Conditions under Which Writing Stopped

Interveners and Interventions

Seeming Effect of Parameters and Variables—established by others; set by self.

Reformulation:

(Same categories as above)

9. Contemplation of Product

Length of Contemplation
Unit Contemplated
Effect of Product upon Self
Anticipated Effect upon Reader

10. Seeming Teacher Influence on Piece

Elements of Product Affected:

Registers—field of discourse; mode of written discourse; tenor of discourse.

Formulation of Title or Topic; Length; Purpose; Audience; Deadline; Amenities; Treatment of Written Outcome; Other.

ters devised by the British linguists Halliday, McIntosh, and Strevens because of the applicability of their category-system to this inquiry.

Registers these linguists define as the varieties of language from which the user of that language makes his oral and written choices.[1] Registers are divided into the following three categories: (1) the field of discourse, or the area of experience dealt with; (2) the mode of discourse, whether the discourse is oral or written; and (3) the tenor of discourse, the degree of formality of treatment.

Although, to the investigator's knowledge, the three linguists do not attempt to specify the various fields of discourse, it seems a refinement helpful for a closer analysis of the composing process. In his essay on poetic creativity, the psychologist R.N. Wilson divides experiences tapped by writers into four categories: (1) encounters with the natural (nonhuman) environment; (2) human interrelations; (3) symbol systems; and (4) self.[2] For the analysis of student writing in this inquiry, "symbol systems" becomes "encounters with induced environments or artifacts."

Another useful refinement of the system of registers is to divide the category "the written mode of discourse" into species. In their speculations on modes of student writing, Britton, Rosen, and Martin of the University of London have devised the following schema:

Modes of Student Writing

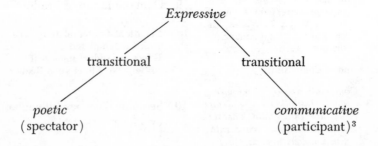

Expressive

transitional   transitional

poetic   *communicative*
(spectator)   (participant)[3]

They regard all writing as primarily expressive—that is, expressing the thoughts and feelings of the writer in relation to some field of discourse. But beyond sheer expressiveness, writing evolves toward, or becomes, one of two major modes: *poetic*, in which the student observes some field of discourse, behaving as a spectator; or *communicative*, in which the student somehow participates through his writing in the business of the world. The many exemplars of writing Britton, Rosen, and Martin regard as mid-mode they have called *transitional* writings. (One longs to give the two kinds of transitional writings exponents, as with Hayakawa's cow[1] and cow[2].)

To this investigator, the notions that all student writings emanate from an expressive impulse and that they then bifurcate into two major modes is useful and accurate. Less satisfactory are the terms assigned to these modes and the implications of these terms about the relation of the writing self to the field of discourse. The terms are at once too familiar and too ultimate. Both *poetic* and *communicative* are freighted with connotations that intrude. *Poetic*, for example, sets up in most minds a contrast with prose, or prosaic, although in this schema the poetic mode includes certain kinds of prose, such as the personal fictional narrative. Second, they are too absolute: rather than describing two general kinds of relations between the writer and his world, they specify absolute states—either passivity or participation.

The following schema seems at once looser and more accurate:

Modes of Student Writing

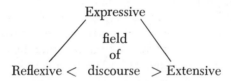

The terms *reflexive* and *extensive* have the virtue of relative unfamiliarity in discussions of modes of discourse. Second, they suggest two general kinds of relations between the writing self and the field of discourse—the *reflexive*, a basically contemplative role: "What does this experience mean?"; the *extensive*, a basically active role: "How, because of this experience, do I interact with my environment?" Note that neither mode suggests ultimate states of passivity or participation. Note too that the mid-modes or transitional writings have been eliminated from this schema as a needless complexity—at this time.

Subcategories can be established as well for the register, "tenor of discourse," which concerns the distance observed between the writing self and field of discourse, expressed by the degree of formality observed in the writing itself. Formality or decorum in written discourse can be established by one or more of the following means: lexical choices, syntactic choices, rhetorical choices. Obviously, the most formal discourse would employ all three means. The next question, of course, is what constitutes decorum for these three means.

Most past and current composition guides have been predicated upon the belief that there are established and widely accepted indices of written decorum and that student writers of all ages can learn and employ them. Levels of diction really refer to corpora of lexical items that are consigned some place on a formality continuum. Syntactically, certain orderings of words are regarded as more formal than others: the "balanced" sentence, for example, as against the "loose" sentence. Rhetorically, certain arrangements of sentences and the kinds of signals that precede and connect them are also regarded as more formal than others; for example, the use of explicit "lead sentences" and explicit transitional devices, such as *nevertheless* and *however*.

The teacher-initiated assignment as stimulus has specifiable dimensions. It occurs within a context that may affect it in certain ways. Included in this context are relationships the student writer may have with his peers or, more importantly—given the teacher-centered nature of very many American classrooms—with his teacher; the general curriculum in English being enacted, and the specific activities in composition of which the assignment is a part; and the other stimuli that have immediately accompanied the assignment, with the sequence and mode of these probably very important. As an example of the last: if a teacher shows a film as stimulus for writing, do her words precede the film, or follow it, or both? Here, as with the other dimensions specified, no research of any consequence has been undertaken.

Internal aspects of the assignment that may bear upon the student's writing process, and product, include the following specifications: (1) registers—the field of discourse, the written mode, and the tenor; (2) the linguistic formulation of the assignment; (3) the length; (4) the purpose; (5) the audience; (6) the deadline; (7) the amenities, such as punctuation and spelling; and (8) the treatment of written outcome —that is, if the teacher plans to evaluate the product, how—by grade? comment? conference? peer response? or by some combination of these?

The reception of the assignment by the student is affected by the following: (1) the general nature of the task, particularly the registers specified; (2) the linguistic formulation of the assignment; (3) the student's comprehension of the task; (4) his ability to enact the task; and (5) his motivation to enact the task. There is now some empirical evidence that not all students can write with equal ease and skill in all modes.[4] For the less able student some species of mode present almost insuperable difficulties—for example, the impersonal argument in which the writer is to present "dispassionately" more than one side, or aspect, of a case. Consequently, if a teacher gives an assignment requiring writing in this sub-mode, certain students may be unable to complete adequately, or even to begin, such an assignment. Along with being intellectively unable to perform the assignment, the student may also be unmotivated or psychically unable to perform the assignment. Such "blocks" may emanate from strikingly different sources: the student may find the task too boring, or he may find the task too threatening. He may not want to write, again, about his summer vacation or the function of Banquo's ghost; or about family life, if his father has just lost his job or if his mother has just threatened divorce.

Next, there are two possible preludes to the act of writing: *prewriting* and *planning*. *Prewriting* is that part of the composing process that extends from the time a writer begins to perceive selectively certain features of his inner and/or outer environment with a view to writing about them—usually at the instigation of a stimulus—to the time when he first puts words or phrases on paper elucidating that perception.

Planning refers to any oral and written establishment of elements and parameters before or during a discursive formulation. Prewriting occurs but once in a writing process; planning can occur many times.

Whether or not a piece of writing is self- or other-initiated affects both prewriting and planning. If the piece is teacher-initiated and if the assignment is highly specific, particularly as to a fairly immediate deadline, it is likely that the prewriting period will be brief—or that the paper will be late. Planning is intricately affected by the nature of the assignment as well. One way of regarding an assignment is as the part the teacher takes in the planning of a piece of writing. If the teacher's part is extensive—as in specifying registers, length, purpose, audience—it is obvious that the part a student plays in his own planning is diminished. There seems to be some evidence that a delicate balance, if not a paradox, exists in the giving of assignments. If the teacher sets too many of the variables for a piece of writing (we need to know far more about how many are too many, and which variables are more significant than others), some students feel too confined, too constricted by the limitations to write "well." If the teacher does not specify enough variables (again, how many are enough, and for what students?), the task may daunt at least some students by its ambiguity or by its degrees of freedom. If there are individual differences here, which students learn from highly specified assignments and which from loose assignments? And if future empirical studies suggest giving more than a single assignment to accommodate these differences in responses, how can the teacher be certain there is some equality in the tasks he assigns? Again, far more research needs to be undertaken in this area of the teaching of composition.

For the phases of prewriting and planning, as in almost every other phase that follows, a category in the outline is "Interveners and Interventions." It is an extremely rare situation for writers, particularly student writers, to proceed from initial stimulus to final draft, or revision, without interruption. Rather, events and people—teachers, notably—intervene; and in major enough ways to affect the process of writing, and the product.

Interveners, for the purposes of this study, will be defined as persons who enter into the composing process of another. For student writers, interveners are most often two sorts of adults, teachers and parents; and one sort of contemporary, a friend. Who intervenes seems related to whether the writing is self-sponsored or school-sponsored, with teacher and parent, expectedly, intervening in school-sponsored writing; friend, in self-sponsored.

Starting is a specifiable moment in the process of writing—and the one perhaps most resistant to logical characterization and analysis. Certain psychoanalytic or certain learning theories provide explanations as to why a writer starts to write. If one accepts the major Freudian metaphor of the tri-partite self, starting can be regarded as the moment when the id, or the unconscious, is, in R.N. Wilson's terms, "the least amenable to ego mastery," and breaks through the controls usually exerted by the ego and super-ego.[5]

Because of the clearly profound, and opaque, nature of this moment, the kinds of elements that can be accurately specified, that exhibit themselves in behavior, are contextual—and, usually, trivial. Examples here are where, physically, the writer is when he begins and what habits or rituals he observes. Perhaps the most significant feature of starting that can be readily observed is what element the writer first places on paper, and where in the finished piece that element occurs, if at all.

For the purposes of this inquiry, eight twelfth graders attempt to compose aloud. The assumption here is that *composing aloud*, a writer's effort to externalize his process of composing, somehow reflects, if not parallels, his actual inner process.

At least three interesting questions can be asked about this particular, and peculiar, form of verbal behavior. First, are there recurring characteristics as one or more persons compose aloud? Second, if so, can a category-system be devised by which these behaviors can be usefully classified? Three, can provocative hypotheses be generated to account for these behaviors?

Composing aloud can be characterized as the alternation of composing behaviors and of hesitation phenomena of various sorts—that is, of verbal behaviors that *directly* pertain to the selection and ordering of components for a piece of written discourse, and those which do not.

Anticipating is different from planning in the following three ways: Planning involves the projection of a total piece of discourse; anticipating, the projection of a portion of discourse. Planning does not occur in the language of the piece; anticipating often employs the exact lexicon and syntax that will appear in the finished piece of discourse.

Finally, anticipating, as Jerome Bruner notes, shuttles between the present and the future; planning does not:

> The speaker or writer rides ahead of rather than behind the edge of his utterance. He is organizing ahead, marshaling thoughts and words and transforming them into utterances, anticipating what requires saying. If the listener is trafficking back and forth between the present and the immediate past, the speaker is principally shuttling between the present and the future. . . . The tonic effect of speaking is that one thrusts the edge of the present toward the future. In one case anticipation is forced into abeyance. In the other it dominates the activity.[6]

Student writers frequently demonstrate the phenomenon of anticipation in their writing as they compose aloud. They anticipate the use of a theme or of an element, then return to the present portion of discourse, to fill out the intervening matter. There are clear signs of efficiently divided attention, as they focus upon the here-and-now while at the same time considering where the future element will eventually, and best, appear.

There are other strategies a writer follows in dealing with the elements or components of discourse: he can accept, and immediately employ, an element; he can accept, then immediately abandon or delete his choice (if too much time intervenes, the action becomes reformulation or revision); or he can combine the element in some way with other elements in the discourse.*

When dealing with syntactic components—and one must note at once that there are also lexical, rhetorical, and imagaic components— these actions correspond to the basic transforming operations—addi-

---

* The kind of self-censoring that eliminates an option before it is uttered is outside the purview of this inquiry.

tion; deletion; reordering or substitution; and combination, especially embedding.[7]

In his article, "Generative Grammars and the Concept of Literary Style," Richard Ohmann gives the following definition of style: "Style is in part a characteristic way of deploying the transformational apparatus of a language."[8] As illustrations, he breaks down passages from Faulkner ("The Bear"), Hemingway ("Soldier's Home"), James ("The Bench of Desolation"), and Lawrence (*Studies in Classic American Literature*) into kernel sentences and notes that, for each, a different cluster of optional transformations is favored. The special "style" of Faulkner, for example, seems partially dependent upon his favoring three transformations: the relative, or wh, transformation, the conjunctive transformation, and the comparative transformation.[9]

There is no reason to believe that nonprofessional writers do not also have their characteristic ways "of deploying the transformational apparatus of a language," although these ways may be less striking, with less reliance on "a very small amount of grammatical apparatus."[10] (Query: when teachers or critics say that a writer has "no style," is what they mean that the writer in question has no strongly favored ways of transforming?)

The next question, of course, becomes why one favors a given cluster of transforms. One explanation seems to be that a writer is following some sort of "program" of style, a series of principles, implied or explicit, of what constitutes "good" writing. For example, he might break the concept "coherence" into a set of behavioral objectives, such as "Be clear about referents" and "Repeat necessary lexical elements."

Composing aloud does not occur in a solid series of composing behaviors. Rather, many kinds of hesitation behaviors intervene.[11] The most common of these are making filler sounds; making critical comments; expressing feelings and attitudes, toward the self as writer, to the reader; engaging in digressions, either ego-enhancing or discourse-related; and repeating elements. Even the student writer's silence can be categorized: the silence can be filled with physical writing (sheer scribal activity); with reading; or the silence can be seemingly "unfilled"—"seemingly" because the writer may at these times be engaged in very important nonexternalized thinking and composing.

The alternation of composing behaviors and of hesitation phenomena gives composing aloud a certain rhythm or tempo. It is interesting to speculate that a writer may have a characteristic tempo of composing, just as he may use a characteristic cluster of transforms.

Composing aloud captures the behaviors of planning and of writing.

Partly because of the very definition of reformulation, and partly because of the attitudes of the twelfth graders toward this portion of the composing process, it does not capture reformulating.

Writing and reformulating differ in significant ways. One is in the role memory is asked to play. Another is in the nature and number of interferences in the two portions of the composing process. In writing, the memory is seldom asked to recall more than the words and the structures in the given unit of discourse upon which the writer is working and, possibly, in the unit immediately preceding. In reformulating, the memory is asked to recall larger units of discourse for longer periods of time, against the "noise" of all intervening experiences. (In writing itself, the major form of "noise" seems to be the physical act of writing, the scribal activity.)

A third way they differ is in the relative roles of encoding and decoding in the two portions of the process. In writing, encoding—the production of discourse—is clearly dominant. Decoding during the act of writing for the most part consists of rereading one's own recently formulated, and remembered, words in short, retrospective scannings. In reformulation, decoding plays a larger role because of the intervention of a longer period of time and the consequent forgetting that has occurred. One becomes more truly the reader, rather than the writer, of a given piece of discourse—that is, he views his writing from the point of view of a reader who needs all possible grammatical and rhetorical aids for his own comprehension.

Reformulation can be of three sorts: correcting, revising, and rewriting. The size of the task involved differs among the three: correcting is a small, and usually trivial, affair that consists of eliminating discrete "mechanical errors" and stylistic infelicities. An other-imposed task, correcting is synonymous with composing in the minds of many secondary and elementary school teachers of composition. Revising is a larger task involving the reformulation of larger segments of discourse and in more major and organic ways—a shift of point of view toward the material in a piece; major reorganizations and restructurings. While others may recommend correcting, the writer himself must accede to the value of the task of revising. Rewriting is the largest of the three, often involving total reformulation of a piece in all its aspects; or the scrapping of a given piece, and the writing of a fresh one.

Stopping represents a specifiable moment—rather, moments—in the writing process because, of course, a writer stops more than once although the final stopping, like the first starting—the first placement of words on a page—has special, or exaggerated, characteristics. One stops at the ends of drafts or versions of a piece of writing; he stops when he thinks the piece is finished—when he feels he has worked through or worked out the possibilities, contentive and formal, that interest him in the piece; he also stops for the purpose of presenting a piece in a given state for the reading—and, usually, evaluation—of one or more others.

These moments and motives for stopping do not necessarily coincide. Again, whether or not a piece of writing is assigned affects stopping as it affects almost every other phase in the writing process. If an imposed deadline forces the writer to submit a piece of writing for reading and evaluation before he is content with his formulation, before he experiences closure, states of tension develop that make the act of stopping painful, if not impossible. Hypothesis: Stopping occurs most "easily" when one's personal sense of closure occurs at the same time as a deadline imposed by oneself or by others.

The next moment to be noted is the *contemplation of product*—the moment in the process when one feels most godlike. One looks upon part, or all, of his creation and finds it—good? uneven? poor? If he has not steadily, or even erratically, kept his reader in mind during the process, the writer may think of him now and wonder about the reception the piece will experience in the world.

The final category concerns the *seeming influence by a teacher* or by a group of teachers upon the piece of student writing. There are five sources of information about this elusive matter of influences: student statement; student practice; teachers' written evaluations of former pieces, if available; student descriptions of composition teaching experienced; and, the most difficult information to obtain, what those composition teachers actually do in the classroom as they "teach" composition.

This chapter represents a theoretical sketch of one of the most complex processes man engages in. Although it is roughly taxonomic, it does not of course purport to be exhaustive. Nonetheless, almost every sentence contains or implies hypotheses upon which one could spend a lifetime in empirical research. Perhaps investigators other than the writer will find here materials for provocative questions and generative hypotheses about the composing process, particularly of students.

CHAPTER 4

LYNN: PROFILE OF A TWELFTH-GRADE WRITER

Context

The community in which Lynn lives is one of the few truly cross-cultural districts within Chicago. The local couplet, like the area, runs "From the mill/To Pill Hill." The mills are the steel mills of South Chicago; near them live, often on relief, blacks and newly arrived Mexicans and Puerto Ricans. "Pill Hill" is the residential area where many Jewish doctors, dentists, and professors live. Between lie several miles of small brick bungalows owned by second generation Polish- and Serbian-Americans. The school district has this approximate ethnic distribution: 16 percent black, 20 percent Polish and Serbian, 24 percent Mexican and Puerto Rican, 40 percent Jewish.

Lynn lives on "Pill Hill," the oldest of four children of a Jewish lawyer. Her mother is a high school history teacher at the same high school Lynn attends (this fact may at least partially explain Lynn's sophistication, hovering near cynicism, about teachers and their ways revealed in her interviews). Her brother is three years younger; her sisters, six and eight-and-a-half years younger. All four of Lynn's grandparents were born in Europe.

Lynn's high school has a proud academic tradition: until recently, in addition to the five tracks common in other Chicago high schools, it had a special Century Club—the top 100 in each class of approximately 550 students. Many senior members of the Century Club, like Lynn, take advanced placement courses and actual college courses at a nearby city junior college; in fact, Lynn's schedule, with its spaced classes and free time, more closely resembles the schedule of a college freshman than that of a high school senior.

In addition to being in the top five percent of her class academically, Lynn is coeditor of the yearbook and a study hall monitor. If her conversation gives an accurate index, by far the most important extracurricular activity, however, is her work as officer of the Midwest Jewish Youth Institute.

Personally, Lynn is very vivacious as well as a very perceptive girl, attuned to herself and her world. She proved an exceptionally interesting subject because of her self-knowledge and her ability to verbalize the process of her thinking and writing.

Prewriting and Nature of Stimulus

For Lynn the length of prewriting period differs markedly for her three pieces, two essays and a poem. The prewriting period for "Profile of a Smile" (see opposite page) is extremely brief—three minutes—probably because this session represents the first the investigator conducts; and in her anxiety she unintentionally hurries the process. It is the first for the subject as well, and their mutual apprehensions tend to reinforce one another. Also, the investigator presents the writing of the first piece as an exercise—in a sense, as if it were a pilot for writing to come—rather than as an integral part of the investigation. Finally, the investigator really supplies the stimulus:

> It can be, you know, well you can have a description of your feelings about the testing on Saturday or you said something about having a new job. Your impressions of the new job.*

Lynn readily accepts this suggestion—"Yeah, the job would probably be a pretty good idea"—and immediately sets about planning: "Now there are a number of ways I could approach it."

The second session is taken up with Lynn's giving her writing autobiography.† At its close the investigator gives the stimulus for the second piece of writing: "Write about a person, idea, or event that especially intrigues you." Lynn immediately produces three possible subjects:

> Is that such as say, I could talk about taking a bus ride downtown . . . you know, I might be able to get something interested [sic], interesting, I was thinking about this . . . tonight we're going to have a bridge game at my house and I've invited two boys that I've both been dating and neither knows that the other's going out with me, that should be interesting. Also, I notice all these queer people on the bus going, like today, these two old ladies got on, they were straight out of *Arsenic and Old Lace*, they had very tall, very spare looking, they must have been in their sixties, their skirts were halfway to their ankles, they looked like something out of the 1930's and they, I thought they were very interesting, occasionally I see like, I think old people are very interesting, to

---

* Unless otherwise noted, the quotations in this chapter come from transcripts of the interviewer's taped sessions with Lynn.

† Because of a scheduling problem, Lynn's second and third sessions were reversed in content from the ordering described on page 30.

Profile of a Smile

After a few days of desperate searching, having just quit my job at Woolworth's sweat shop, I walked into a warm-looking yellow-and-orange dress shop on East Randolph. My anticipations of a cosy atmosphere were dispelled when I was greeted by a wall of frigid air from the hard-working air conditioner.

I was directed by a frigid sales-lady to the hard-working manager at his desk in the back. The first thing that struck me about Mr. Hobeck was his resemblance to the next-door neighbor on the old Burns and Allen television series. I spent the rest of the interview trying to remember that character's name, but could only come up with the fact that he sold Goodyear tires. Mr. Hobeck had the friendly smile of a practiced salesman which I was not going to let fool me, because those smiles often had the words "we're not hiring" right behind them. The first clue that all this affability was not put-on came when he said that they were hiring summer help. Throughout the interview, which lasted some time and involved a personal questionaire and a rather complicated mathematics test, Mr. Hobeck's smile remained a constant.

This smile has not once left his face in the two weeks I have worked with him and I have thought of three possible causes. The first one is that Mr. Hobeck suffers from a peculiar disease that will not let the muscles of his face turn into a frown. The second is that he is a man of extreme endurance and superior salesmanship which forces him to smile in all situations. The last, and most probable, is that he is a person who really enjoys his work and lets this show through to others.

watch them, and see what they do, little kids too . . . I might be able to get something, just from, some of the people I work with or some of the people who come into the store I could, take one of them.

At the beginning of the next session, which does not occur until two weeks later because of a holiday in the intervening week, Lynn adds two new possible subjects, Snoopy and her grandmother:

Last week I had said how I noticed how I always think old people on the bus and everything were very interesting. And my grandmother stayed with us for the weekend and it sort of struck me that she was a lot older than she used to be and I thought this might be an interesting topic. I could write about that, it's probably the best of the lot.

Note that two of the possible four topics involve Lynn: her grandmother and the two boys; that the fields of discourse in these cases would be the two categories of *self* and *human relationships;* and that the mode if she wrote about either might well be the *reflexive.* The other two subjects of the old ladies on the bus and Snoopy could be handled at a greater distance, with less self-involvement. Lynn chooses Snoopy, the cardboard dog. Why?

Both at the beginning and at the end of the third session Lynn speaks about why she decides against writing about the boys and about her grandmother. One ostensible reason for not writing about the boys is that such a "story" would be too limited in audience appeal: that it would please only girls who read such magazines as *Seventeen.* A second is that the subject is trite: "Oh, I'm sure everybody has had a boyfriend at some time in their life. . . . It's easy to get trite when you're talking about [boys]." Lynn's ostensible reason for not writing about her grandmother is that her grandmother's visit to their home is now two weeks away and no longer fresh in her memory. When the investigator asks her if there are other reasons, Lynn says "the Snoopy thing" is "easier" to write about:

To write about my grandmother one thing that really struck me was when she would sit down in a chair she would sort of almost fall into it and my mother would sort of watch her when she was going up the stairs because they don't have stairs at her house, and this had never occurred to me before that she was rather old. And it would be kind of hard to formulate an entire theme. If I would have perhaps seen her again this week or, I didn't see too many old people on the buses going downtown either which would have given me some insight. No, this is the easiest thing to write about.

The interesting question here is to define what for Lynn is an "easy" subject and what is a "hard" one. Clearly, an "easy" one is a nonpersonal subject, one that does not demand interacting with her feelings, one that is *not* reflexive.

There is evidence from her writing autobiography that this is a fair, if partial, interpretation. At the beginning of her account of high school writing, Lynn says:

> I found that if I could write about a specific incident, and use, specific facts, I was doing a lot better than if I just had to write about like my ambitions . . . I'm sure we had to do a composition on that theme, ah . . . it was very hard, it still is very hard for me to write about abstract things like feelings about something, I do a lot better when I have facts.

Note she defines feelings as "abstract things."

Later in the same session, the investigator asks Lynn why she thinks she feels more comfortable writing about facts rather than feelings. At first she claims she has no idea and changes the subject; later she admits that she finds expressing her feelings painful:

> I've always . . . I've always had trouble talking to people about, my feelings on something. I can quote from other people I can . . . talk about, ahm . . . I can talk about facts more easily than I can talk about abstract things . . . when . . . I was at this Institute, one of the kids kept saying, 'Lynn, you know, you're a great kid but you know it doesn't come out in our discussion group because you seem to be talking in clichés, you never seem to be talking about yourself, about your own feelings, you seem to be giving examples all the time,' I don't know why this is, I could, get some sort of explanation, rather I'm sure, but I don't know.

The investigator then asks if Lynn writes about her feelings when an audience, such as teachers or peers, are not involved: the purpose of the question is to try to discover if Lynn ever engages in private self-sponsored writing, such as diary or journal writing. Lynn then describes two occasions when she has written because she "felt very strongly about something." In both cases, she says she has written these pieces because "there was nobody I could talk to."

Lynn is clearly discomfited by her difficulty in expressing feelings, both in speaking and in writing. She is almost vehement about trying to avoid clichés in her writing, the clichés that her perceptive friend in the quotation above identifies as a defense against the expression of actual emotion. One way of interpreting Lynn's effort to eliminate clichés is as a struggle to find feeling and to express it in her writing.

That her grandmother is moving toward death deeply distresses Lynn; she has difficulty examining her feelings about it, even at the distance of writing about the old ladies on the bus—clearly surrogates for her grandmother. In choosing Snoopy, the cardboard dog, she chooses the subject of the four least requiring emotions from her, although the decision makes her feel guilty.

To suggest that fear of feeling is the sole, or even the predominant, reason for Lynn's choice of topics is not just; her own behavior reveals that the factor of time—more specifically, the amount of time available to her for musing during the prewriting period—strongly affects her choice of subject matter. The relatively swift response which the design of this study requires and her own schedule, too full of distractions, both obviate against her choosing a subject that requires time and quiet.

She is not wholly unwilling to write about the two boys or her grandmother; in fact, for her third piece of writing she says, "I might be able to write on one of these other two topics I was talking about." She chooses poetry rather than the short story as her form "because short stories involve a good plot and I find it hard to invent plots and poetry would be easier."

Her poem "Simplicity, Please" deals, in its original version, with one of the two boys (see opposite page). The question here is why she again chooses the subject of the boy over that of her grandmother. Once more, the factor of time seems significant. At the last session, during which Lynn describes the background to the poem, she says that she first began thinking about the matter in April, four months earlier. The subject of the boy has had a chance to ripen, to deepen; the subject of her grandmother has not.

Lynn's accounts of the prewriting periods of all three pieces lead to the following hypothesis: The length of the prewriting period available affects the choice of subject matter. If, according to the writer's perception, the period is curtailed by his own schedule or by others, he usually does not elect to work on a topic or problem he regards as cognitively or psychically complex. Rather, he chooses one he perceives as more "programmable"—that is, one that corresponds with some kind of schema he has already learned or been taught, and one he has internalized. For Lynn, as for most older secondary students in American schools, this schema is for some kind of extensive expository writing that does not require the deep personal engagement of the writer.

The linguist Leon A. Jakobovits suggests that "stale art" is algorithmic—that is, it is produced by a known algorithm, "defined as a computational device that specifies the order and nature of the steps to be followed in the generation of a sequence."[1] One could say that

First Draft
"Simplicity, Please"

Today
▸ I wish the world were black and white
And white and black,
And laid out neatly
In checkerboard boxes.
The grays ~~are confusing~~.
        (confuse me)

Today I wish that ~~world were~~ there was hate and
(But more love)   love
And nothing
In between.

For today I am in the grays,
And hate and love are so mixed up
In this giant mixmaster of life
That I am afraid to choose;
A wrong choice.

"I set before thee the Blessing
And the 'Curse'"
I don't know which is which.

But lacking that
I think he is afraid to love,
For he's been hurt before.

Final Draft

Simplicity, Please

Today I wish the world were black and white
And white and black,
And laid out neatly
In checkerboard boxes.
The grays are confusing.

Today I wish that there was ~~hate~~ and ~~hate~~ love,
(But more. love)
And nothing
In between.
(But especially love.)

For today I am in the grays,
And love and hate are so mixed up
In the giant Mixmaster
That I am afraid to choose
A wrong choice.

"I set before thee the Blessing
"And the Curse."
I don't know which is which.

the major kind of essay too many students have been taught to write in American schools is algorithmic, or so mechanical that a computer could readily be programmed to produce it: when a student is hurried or anxious, he simply reverts or regresses to the only program he knows, as if inserting a single card into his brain.

Planning

The length of time Lynn spends upon the initial planning for the two prose pieces is quite brief; for the poem, nonexistent. The reason for Lynn's spending only three minutes planning how she will approach "Profile of a Smile" may be attributable to the circumstances under which she and others have been asked to write in school. This may account also for the brevity of the prewriting period.

What happens, however, when Lynn is relatively unrestricted in the time she can spend contemplating and planning a piece of prose? If her approach to "Terpsichordean Greetings" is representative, she spends whatever additional time she has or is given in contemplation, but not in planning. Rather, she still does her planning, as with "Profile of a Smile," immediately before writing.

There are other similarities in her planning for these two pieces. For both, as was shown above, she considers several organizational options—three, in each case. For both, as was also shown above, she considers a personal approach—that is, writing in the reflexive mode— then decides to write extensively, and impersonally, instead.

For both, her planning is oral, not written. Why this absence of written prefiguring? First, both are relatively short pieces of writing (289 and 279 words respectively); and as the pilot study in chapter 1 demonstrates, able students engage in very little written prefiguring for pieces of 500 words or fewer. By not planning in any written form, Lynn proceeds like her peers who participated in the pilot study. As she puts it in her writing autobiography:

> I've never done outlines for compositions which, might help me, some-times . . . if in this, course when I was a sophomore, I would write down two or three points and I'd put them in what order, like one two three four and then I'd put two where four was, and things like that.

and

> Planning, I've never really done much, really. I plan it more in my head and then put it down.

For both pieces of writing she attempts to project the scope of the whole piece and, indeed, does. What she says she will include in "Terpsichordean Greetings," for example, she does include (see page opposite); and in the order she describes:

> This morning I had an idea to write about this thing we got from my sister who is on vacation with our cousins. She sent us from, it might have been Disneyland, a two-foot-high cut-out of Snoopy, the Peanuts dog dancing, and my mother set it up in the middle of the living room so you see it when you walk in the front door. And I thought it might be interesting to write about people's reactions to it, there have been quite a few. And I was thinking of, I had two extremes in mind. This one boy when he walked in the door sort of curled up his nose at it, and I could just hear him thinking, my how gauche can you get. (laughs) And one of my girl friends came and she picked up the thing and she said, "Oh I love Snoopy," and she hugs it, this piece of cardboard. (laughs) Those are two extremes and my mother had a suggestion, well what about the adults who walk in and pretend not to see it, and that might be interesting.

Lynn's approach to "Simplicity, Please," the only poem in this sample, differs in one major way from her approaches to her prose pieces in that she engages in no planning, oral or written, for the poem. In this respect, her practice—or nonpractice—matches that of the professional poets cited in chapter 1. Since many poems, particularly lyric poems, have fewer than 500 words, perhaps the factor of length is more significant than the factor of genre in accounting for the absence of planning.

Starting

For Lynn, starting to write presents a paradox. Her *decision* to begin is a swift, and seemingly painless, one. Her *enactment* of a first sentence, however, is an arduous, even a tortuous, matter; and the actual time expended upon its formulation with both prose pieces is as long as that spent on any sentence—ten minutes for "Terpsichordean Greetings," seven for "Profile of a Smile."

For "Profile of a Smile," after a digression designed to assure the investigator and/or herself that she is intelligent (an evaluation the investigator had already made independently), Lynn says simply, "I think I'll start chronologically. Should I sort of read what I'm writing?" For "Terpsichordean Greetings," once she has established the scope of the piece, she begins:

> . . . this Snoopy [thing] might be interesting if I could think of enough

Terpsichordean Greetings

One of the last things someone would expect to find in a livingroom with walnut-paneled, book-lined walls would be a very large cardboard statue of Snoopy, the Peanuts dog. But in our livingroom anything is possible. He dances with an expression of utter bliss on his face, his arms held open in greeting directly in the path of anyone entering the front door.

Since he is unavoidable, all visitors to our house must register some sort of reaction. My girlfriend Barbara, who also holds her arms open in greeting to the world, embraced Snoopy in all his cardboard cuddliness and cooed, "Isn't he sweet?" The cardboard did not hug her back. My youngest sister does not lavish affection on him although they do carry on some rather interesting, if one-sided, conversations about their mutual enemy, the cat.

Friends of my parents pretend that they don't see Snoopy, politely ignoring what they consider sloppy housekeeping on my mother's part. On the contrary, it was she who put him there, and when she proudly draws attention to his presence the women coo like Barbara and think, "How quaint" and their husbands mutter an embarrassed, "Well, isn't that nice."

The only person who gave a completely sincere reaction was my current beau Marc who stalked into the house, stopped, curled his lip, gave Snoopy his best Jonathan Brewster stare and haughtily said "How gauche can you get!" Alas, poor Marc, you and all the others will never observe Snoopy's credo "To dance is to live; to live is to dance." There are very few dancers in my world.

examples. You know, I think I'm right about that? Now, did you want me to start writing?

In a personal letter to the investigator, the psychologist Jerome Bruner once commented that he was awed at the ease with which his children, then in high school, began writing. They simply sat down, and began. Bruner ends his paragraph: "Writing is for me no ordinary task."

For many adult professional writers, as for Bruner, starting to write represents so awesome a moment that they experience blocks, deterrents that can last, as in the case of Rilke, twenty years or more. Why does Lynn begin so matter-of-factly?

The reason seems linked to the reason for her choosing the subject of Snoopy, the cardboard dog, over that of her grandmother. The time allocated for her writing, by adults whom she is dutiful and disciplined enough to want to please, does not allow her to behave otherwise. She is not permitted to have blocks, as adults are. One can readily imagine what would have happened to Lynn if she had said to one or more of the teachers she describes in her writing autobiography, "I'm sorry; I have a block and can't write today." Or "Please give me another topic; I just can't write on this one." Or "I need more time if I'm to deal with this subject the way I want and feel."

As with the choice of topic, too, her own schedule does not permit her to have blocks. Along with being an extremely amiable girl, Lynn is extremely efficient and well-organized: in fact, no form of American society requires for success from its members more cognitive and psychic versatility and organization than the American high school—and Lynn, assuredly, is one of the successful ones. Lynn must fit widely disparate activities into a limited number of hours, even during her summer vacation: there is no time for mooning or moping or any form of temperament. Writing is a task to be done like any other, and one simply gets on with it.

With all three pieces, Lynn begins at the beginning: at no time, even with the poem, does she proceed from a Valeryian "ligne donée," a word, phrase, or clause that will ultimately appear in other than the initial position. This initial left-to-right thrust of composing—this "marching-through-Georgia" effect—holds for the overall rhetorical organization of the pieces. Once into the piece, certain recursive movements, certain pendulum actions, occur; but Lynn enters the material once and once only, from a given vantage; and she does not go outside again to consider another route in.

Composing Aloud: A Characterization

Certain general statements can be made about Lynn's process of writing as she composes aloud. The first is that her dealings with smaller segments of discourse like the sentence and her dealings with a total piece of writing resemble one another. Both, obviously, involve the selection and arrangement of elements—lexical, syntactic, imagaic. Less obviously, there are in the parts as in the whole the same discernible portions of projecting, formulating, and reformulating.

The second is that Lynn, like the professional writers discussed by Richard Ohmann, has characteristic ways "of deploying the transformational apparatus of a language."[2] She, too, relies heavily upon "a very small amount of grammatical apparatus."[3]

Third, there seem to be certain stylistic principles operating to affect, even govern, Lynn's choices of transforms. Indeed, Lynn seems to follow some sort of "program" of style, a program whose origins can be partially traced. This program affects not only her dealings with syntax, but with lexis, rhetoric, and imagery as well.

Finally, the composing does not occur as a left-to-right, solid, uninterrupted activity with an even pace. Rather, there are recursive, as well as anticipatory, features; and there are interstices, pauses involving hesitation phenomena of various lengths and sorts that give Lynn's composing aloud a certain—perhaps a characteristic—tempo.

Projecting—Anticipating

With both prose pieces, Lynn anticipates major later portions of discourse. With "Profile of a Smile," after she refers to the smile of the manager, she foresees, essentially, the rest of her description:

> Yeah, I can sort of wrap it up here by saying like, 'Throughout the interview which involved the math test blah, blah, blah'—ah, 'he still remained sunny,' and then I can just say, 'after having worked there for two week's he's still smiling and for anyone to have a phony smile for that long, he's either got terrific endurance, or he's sincere.' Then I could end it right there.

Very early in the composing of "Terpsichordean Greetings," Lynn anticipates her use of Snoopy's motto which will eventually become the second-to-last sentence in her twelve-sentence essay:

> . . . something about 'it is hard to describe the utter bliss that is on this dog's face' if you've ever seen the picture of the dancing where they have 'to live is to dance, to dance is to live.'

A short while later, she speaks about the motto once again, this time in conjunction with her friend Barbara:

> She [Barbara] remembered the motto that, uhm, the Snoopy sweat-shirts have, this same picture of Snoopy.

In fact, it is accurate to suggest that for Lynn almost all major elements that fuse to form both essays seem present, from a very early moment in the composing process, within the foreconsciousness of the writer. (The significant exception may be Lynn's finest act of rhetoric—the last sentence of "Terpsichordean Greetings.")

Kinds of Transformational Operations

How does Lynn build a sentence? Here she is engaged in con-structing the second sentence of "Terpsichordean Greetings":

> *He dances in front**
> *He dances*
> *He dances in front of the living room*
> *He dances* (sixteen-second pause)
> *He dances with an expression of utter bliss on his face,* I could say "smack in the middle of the" (three-second pause)
> *He dances with an expression of utter bliss on his face directly in the path of anyone*—yes, this is going to be good—*entering the front door* . . .
> Now I think I can put something else in that sentence about 'He dances' (rereads silently)
> I might make it, "He dances with an expression of utter bliss on his face, his arms held open in greeting, directly in the path, et cetera"

If this sentence is divided into Christensen's "levels," it can be set out as follows:

> 1 He dances
>   2 with an expression of utter bliss on his face (Prepositional phrase)
>   3 his arms held open in greeting (Absolute)
>   4 directly in the path of anyone (Prepositional phrase)
>   5 entering the front door (Verb cluster)

As with many other sentences in these pieces, the architectonics of this sentence involves many major forms of transforming operations. One could say that the essential, or base, operation is that of a right-branching addition: that the movement of the sentence is essentially left-to-right.

But there are also recursive, and endocentric, features: first the ad-

---

* Italic type denotes what Lynn wrote.

verb *smack* is inserted; later the noun absolute *his arms held open in greeting* is inserted prior to *directly in the path.*

There are exact grammatical substitutions: the single adverb *smack* is replaced by the single adverb *directly.*

There is an expansion: the juxtaposed prepositional phrases *in front of the living room* become the juxtaposed prepositional phrases *plus* the participial phrase *entering the front door.*

Lynn does not employ all transforming operations with equal frequency. There are favored operations; for example, embeddings involving the construction of the appositive and of compound adjectives. The combining of two bases into compound adjectives is one of the few transforming actions that occurs in slow and externalized motion.

In "Profile of a Smile," for example, Lynn describes the shop:

> It was all yellow and everything as you walk into this (ten-second pause) you know. It was yellow and orange. Could I hyphenate yellow and orange if I want? (writing) . . . It will make the construction better. *I walked into a warm-looking yellow-and-orange dress shop on East Randolph.*

Here is the movement from base sentences to predicate adjective to pre-noun compound adjectives:

> The shop was yellow.
> The shop was orange.
> The shop was yellow and orange.
> The yellow-and-orange dress shop.

Lynn is aware not only of using, but of over-using, this construction. Referring to the compound adjective *yellow-and-orange,* she says, "I love my hyphenated adjectives." Referring to the double compound *book-lined, walnut-paneled,* she says more critically, "I don't like the construction. I use it too much, I think."

Style

There seems to be in Lynn's writing the operation of a "program" in style: that is, there seems to be a series of stylistic principles that direct Lynn's choices among options. Thanks to a revelation in her writing autobiography, one can discern the source of this "program" that directs many, if not most, of Lynn's choices. Near the end of her autobiography, Lynn refers to a three-part directive reiterated many times by her otherwise forgettable eleventh-grade teacher:

one thing last year in our English course she said, "your writing should be clear concise and memorable," those were our key words

That these words affect her explicitly is seen as she composes aloud "Profile of a Smile." She refers to this teacher as she shortens *he did the Goodyear tires commercial* to *he sold Goodyear tires:*

> I had an English teacher who was always telling us to be concise, and she loved Melville who was anything but concise. But I guess I'm no Melville so I'll have to make it concise.

Analysis of what Lynn does as she composes aloud reveals that her behavior can be interpreted as efforts to enact the first two parts of this directive (Lynn seems, sensibly, to treat the third part—the production of memorable prose—as overambitious), according to her own operational definitions of these abstractions.

Not only do Lynn's efforts to be clear and concise affect her dealings with syntax; they affect as well her dealings with (1) lexical, (2) rhetorical, and (3) imagaic components.

(1) For example, in "Profile of a Smile" Lynn can be seen revising earlier elements to prevent exact lexical repetition. In the first paragraph, she changes *shop* in the first sentence to *store:* "Just make this 'store,' in the sentence before, because I think 'shop' would sound better." In the second paragraph she uses the store manager's name in the fourth sentence because "[I've] already said 'manager.'" It is as if Lynn is heeding the implicit, misguided directive: "One way of achieving clarity is not to use the same word twice if a synonym or antecedent can be found."

(2) Despite her efforts to achieve concision, Lynn produces, as noted above, a number of grammatically intricate sentences—and these worry her. Her concern takes the form of attempting consciously at times a short and relatively untransformed sentence. Lynn says, as she composes the sentence *But in our living room anything is possible,* "just make a short sentence to relieve after all of that,"—"that" being the first intricate sentence of "Terpsichordean Greetings."*

(3) Lynn tries to arrange subtle and imaginative transitions through patterns of imagery. In fact, she is so concerned with shaping such transitions that she is willing to sacrifice both her overall plan for the piece and verisimilitude to achieve them.

As she works on the imagaic transition achieved by the double use

---

* Another explanation for the short sentence could be sheer fatigue: transforming the former sentence, a first sentence, has taken a great deal of energy; and Lynn is giving herself a respite.

of *frigid* and *hard-working* at the beginning of "Profile of a Smile," she realizes she is changing the nature of her essay: "This isn't turning out to be, this isn't turning out as a character. . . ." But she continues shaping the transition. Later, she sacrifices verisimilitude:

> Now I could lie a little and say "it was a complicated mathematics test and Mr. H——'s smile remained a constant." I'll do that. It sounds better even though it's not true.

Such shaping of transitions can be regarded as a response to her teacher's three-part directive since it is clear that the succinctness achieved through imagaic transitions is yet another means of achieving concision.

Other Observed Behaviors

Observed behaviors, as noted in chapter 3, can be divided into silent activities and vocalized hesitation phenomena. The three kinds of silent activity are physical writing, silent reading, and "unfilled" pauses. Vocalized hesitation phenomena or filled pauses consist of filler sounds, expressions of feelings and attitudes, digressions, and repetition of elements.

Silent Activities

By examining Appendix B, which indicates at what points Lynn is actually putting pen or pencil to paper, one can note that there is no regular pattern of when scribal activity occurs in relation to oral composing. (See pages 129-136.) At times Lynn writes an element at the same time she first utters it; at times she writes the element after she has uttered it a number of times. At times the element is just a word or a phrase; at times she waits, then writes a fairly long complex sentence straight through—for example, the eleventh sentence of "Terpsichordean Greetings."

Scribal activity seems also to function as an intrusive form of "noise" in the composing process. At one point Lynn notes as she is writing, "I forgot what I was going to say." At another, she forgets to write down the phrase, *of my parents,* which she has already spoken; and she makes the comment, "I think faster than I write." If oral anticipating thrusts the discourse forward, as Bruner suggests, the physical act of writing may be said, on the other hand, to pull it back.

Reading is for Lynn another kind of hesitation phenomena. This activity usually occurs when Lynn comes to the end of a group of sentences she regards as a paragraph:

> I want to read this part over again; I think I might start a new paragraph.

> I will read the whole thing through, the whole paragraph.

and

> . . . I'm reading over that last paragraph. I have to think of a better ending.

Lynn's behaviors here suggest that her operational definition of a paragraph is "that segment of discourse at the end of which I pause and read." In his article "A Discourse-Centered Rhetoric of the Paragraph," Paul C. Rodgers, Jr., notes what he finds as the only universal characteristic of paragraphs:

> About all we can usefully say of *all* paragraphs at present is that their authors have marked them off for special considerations as *stadia of discourse*, in preference to other stadia, other patterns, in the same material. 'At this point,' the writer tells us with his indentation, 'a major stadium of discourse has just been completed. Rest for a moment, recollect and reconsider, before the next begins.'[4]

If one were to continue the quotation on the basis of Lynn's paragraphing behavior, it might read:

> . . . 'Rest for a moment, recollect and consider' just as I the writer did when I was composing.

Once again, the data suggest that later reader behavior parallels the behavior of the original reader, the writer himself, as he composed.

Vocalized Hesitation Phenomena

Lynn seldom fills pauses with filler sounds: both her spontaneous speech and her "composing" speech are usually free of [m], [ɜ], and [e]. On two occasions when she uses "Hmm," the syllable qualifies as an interjection rather than as a filler sound.

At times she employs morphemes of low semantic content. There are instances of the use of "et cetera," "blah, blah, blah," and "such-and-such" to fill pauses. Each seems to serve a different function. "Et cetera" occurs at the end of a segment and suggests there, as it conventionally does, that the material to follow will be treated as the material that preceded. "Blah, blah, blah" is a semantically empty surrogate for a meaningful morpheme that will fill the given spaces within the utterance later. The single instance of "such-and-such" is a substitute for "Woolworth's," a name Lynn cannot for the moment remember because her attention seems focused on a more immediate composing problem. A more characteristic set of "fillers" Lynn employs is the use of phrases of low semantic content. Commonly used are "let's see," "something about," "still can't think," "How can I phrase that?"

Statements revealing one's attitudes toward his own skills and abilities while composing, as during other activities, can be arranged along a continuum from self-congratulation to self-denigration (intervening "stages" would be self-acceptance, neutrality, ambivalence, self-criticism).

If Lynn's statements about herself as she writes the two pieces of prose (she makes none toward herself as poet) are placed along this continuum, a few qualify as self-congratulatory (3); many as self-accepting (12); almost none as neutral or ambivalent (1); some as self-critical (8); and none as self-denigrating.

Lynn is not often self-congratulatory; but occasionally her ingenuity in solving an immediate writing problem delights her: "Now this gives me a tie-in to relate to different people's reactions. Hmm, that's pretty clever"; and " 'Alas'—oh, this is good!" Her most frequent comments indicate self-acceptance and willingness to try. There are three main verbal indices for this category: "Yeah," "Okay," and "I can." Lynn demonstrates here at the same time tentativeness and commitment, a polarity of traits often present in creative activity: "It might be too complex but I'll see what I come up with" and "This is sort of a digression but I think it's okay because it brings in a sort of different point."

She is self-questioning somewhat less frequently. A few of the questions are clearly directed to the investigator; when this is the case and the question trivial, the investigator responds nondirectively:

L: Could I hyphenate yellow and orange if I want?
I: If you want.

When she abandons an option, she is occasionally forceful in her displeasure—"No, no, no"; but her displeasure with herself is mild as it is rare—for example, "But I don't like it [the title] so much."

The profile Lynn gives through these comments, then, is that of an extremely poised, assured, and open writer, occasionally skeptical about what she has done or what she plans to do, but never so negative about a specific piece of work nor of her ability in general that she stops trying in disgust or defeat. Her ego-strength seems great enough for her to believe that she can complete any assigned writing task, not only adequately but skillfully enough to please herself and her evaluator, whoever the evaluator may be.

Lynn proceeds as if what she writes will find an audience—and one wider than a single teacher or investigator. Note her use of *everyone* in the following sentence: "I don't know if everyone who reads this would get the implication." She also seems to consider it part of her writing task to pique and maintain the interest of her readers. She chooses not to write a story about her current social difficulties with one of two young men: "that wouldn't be too interesting to anyone else." Later, she enlarges the scope of the possible audience for her story:

> It might be interesting to write something just to earn money for it but they're not that interesting really, they have a limited audience appeal. This magazine [*Seventeen*] is aimed at high school aged girls and those are the only people who'd be interested in this sort of a story.

Clearly, Lynn wants, and expects, to be read.

Earlier, it was shown that Lynn's major objective as she wrote was to enact her eleventh grade teacher's directive, to be clear, concise, and memorable. All three parts of this directive really emanate from a concern for the reader. That Lynn tries so assiduously to heed them is probably the best index of her profound concern for her reader.

Of the two possible kinds of self-imposed interruptions to the writing process, blocks and digressions, we have already seen that Lynn does not experience blocks because she does not attempt over-difficult tasks. Lynn does, however, experience digressions, which can be defined either as a diversion initiated by the writer to take him temporarily away from a writing problem or as a nonproductive effort at anticipation.

There are essentially two types of digressions Lynn engages in: the first, extrinsic and ego-enhancing; the second, discourse-related. Here is a series of ego-enhancing digressions; the first two appear in the first session; the third, in the third session:

> (1) When I walked into the store for the first time, I'd never heard of the place and I went looking for the manager and he . . . said, 'How are you?' and 'You look very bright.'
>
> (2) Now this is really getting off the track but I think it was very in-

teresting. The test was, it was like a standardized test. It was printed out and with multiple choice answers but the questions were so ridiculous . . . like 'If something was selling three for eighty-eight' or something like that. You know, 'how much would one thing be,' you know,' simple math problems. But they had really stupid questions, I thought they were stupid. . . . They would have a list of proverbs. . . . I got all of those wrong, but I got all of the math questions right so I got the job. Let's see how can I phrase it about the proverbs?

(3) The thing about our living room, there are more books and magazines there than, that's no, really not so many books because there are boxes of books in the basement. . . . There are magazines galore.

Lynn's third digression, for example, is to assure the investigator that she comes from a literate household, or at least from one in which there are not only books but "magazines galore." The purpose of the first digression is to show the investigator that others find her bright, with the implicit causal question, "Therefore why shouldn't you?" The second is a little more complex. Lynn seems to need to confess to the investigator that she did not do well on a verbal test (the proverbs test), perhaps so that there is no feeling she is involved in the inquiry under the false pretenses of being a highly able verbal student. At the same time, she also needs reassurance that the test itself was stupid, or at least misleading. She not only gives herself this reassurance; but she fuses the difficult verbal test with a mathematics test in which she did well, to neutralize its effect.

In addition to this kind of digression, the motivation of which Lynn seems unaware, there are others where she seems to understand why she makes a certain writing decision: "I find it hard to do dialogue because all my characters end up speaking like me which is not really good because that's not how they talk."

Her final digression is to explain an allusion, not unlike a footnote in "The Waste Land":

gave Snoopy his best Jonathan Brewster, now I don't know if you, Jonathan Brewster is the Frankenstein nephew in *Arsenic and Old Lace*. He [Marc] played him in a play, it was excellent.

As this section reveals, Lynn engages in very few digressions unrelated to the writing of the two prose pieces. When she does, her usual purpose seems to be to win the approval of, or to inform, the investigator.

An example of a digression which might be defined as a nonproductive anticipation is Lynn's dealings with the family cat in "Terpsichordean Greetings." She has just finished formulating the sentence, *Even my youngest sister does not lavish affection on him, although she does carry on some rather interesting, if one-sided, conversations about their mutual enemy, the cat.* The cat stimulates his own chain of associations:

> Now I could talk about what the cat does. Perhaps the cat realizes that Snoopy is a dog and therefore dislikes him, or perhaps she's jealous that people seem to pay more attention to him when they walk in the door. But she sort of gives it a whack with a paw when she walks by. My father pretends to hate the cat. He will fake a kick when he walks by and stamp his foot. That's sort of what the cat's doing to Snoopy.

At last she realizes how far she has moved from her consideration of human reactions to Snoopy. She says, laughing, "That's an entirely different story. I think I can just drop the cat."

Lynn does not seem to be victimized by the irrelevant as some writers are. She sees clearly that she has moved away from the subject of her piece and that the material generated does not belong. Matter-of-factly, she does "just drop the cat" and move back to her prior material and organization.

The Tempo of Composing

Composing aloud as a process consists of the alternation of actual composing behaviors (the selection and ordering of elements) and of all hesitation phenomena the writer employs. Hesitations can consist of a single behavior of the sort noted in the section above or of a series of aligned behaviors, in various combinations. For example, the following sequence

> the *Peanuts dog* (pause) just make a short sentence to relieve after all of that

consists of scribal activity + unfilled pause + "empty" phrase.

Another way of putting the matter is that a hesitation extends from one piece of composing behavior to the next. The hesitation may be very brief, of several seconds' duration, or very long, of several minutes' duration.

With what, if anything, does the length of hesitation correlate? The recent work of two verbal behaviorists provides a double hypothesis to examine with the data. The first is the general conclusion presented by the psychologist Frieda Goldman-Eisler that for spontaneous speech "hesitation pauses precede a sudden increase of information, estimated in terms of transition probabilities."[5] The second is the assumption that George A. Miller tests experimentally and reports in "Some Psychological Studies of Grammar": "the more complicated a grammatical transformation the longer it will take people to perform it."[6]

If composing aloud can be characterized in ways comparable with spontaneous speech, the following two hypotheses may obtain:

> (1) In composing aloud, a specialized form of verbal behavior, hesitation pauses precede a sudden increase of information as represented by grammatical transformations of varying complexity;
> (2) The writer requires longer pauses to perform more complex transformations.

Unfortunately, an analysis of the data yields only the grossest distinctions in the time Lynn requires for performing given transformations. For example, the appositives in the two prose pieces with one exception take an imperceptible amount of time—that is, less than a second. Left-branching additions, such as *Since he is unavoidable,* require, on the other hand, an average of twenty seconds to perform. No accurate statements can be made about other transforming operations Lynn performs because of the grossness of the study. Assuredly, a study of a finer calibration with more careful recording techniques would be useful in ascertaining if some kind of hierarchy can be established for transforming operations performed during composing aloud, for a single writer or for a given group of writers.

Reformulating; Stopping; Contemplating the Product

Reformulating, stopping, and contemplating the product are treated here in a single section because in Lynn's process of writing they take up so little chronological and psychological time that they almost coalesce into a single barely occurring experience.

Partially because of the design and the conduct of this inquiry—but, seemingly, far more because of her attitude toward revising—Lynn does not really reformulate any of the three pieces she writes. There are several features of the design and Lynn's attitudes toward the sessions that may explain, at least in the cases of the two prose pieces, why she does not. Of prime importance is the fact that the design does not explicitly provide for reformulation, an activity which requires quiet, if not solitude; leisure; and some separation in time from the act of writing.

The investigator neither states nor suggests that Lynn revise, nor does she make a direct offer for Lynn to take her piece away so that she can reformulate. Lynn, perhaps consequently (and perhaps like the investigator), treats the sessions as self-contained units to which she allocates, roughly, ninety minutes per session, and in which she devotes her energy to the central writing act. And although there are no verbal data to corroborate the investigator's intuitions on this matter, Lynn behaves as if the investigator, like herself, has a view of the writing process as a no-nonsense, no-dawdle task to which one devotes a given amount of time, and no more.

Lynn's attitudes toward reformulating seem to emanate from her experiences with school writing. In her writing autobiography Lynn makes clear why she "never took it on myself to rewrite a composition":

> Partly because it seemed to be punishment work we were just said [sic], if you have more than so many mistakes, you have to rewrite your composition and it has to be in by Friday after, and . . . she never would . . . our English teachers never re-r---, I mean, maybe she talked to me about my composition I don't remember but I never remember any suggestions which inspired me, to rewrite something, so that there was any change in the, so that it was any better, the only changes seemed to be technical ones.

First, although it is clear from her responses that Lynn understands the term *revise*, she never uses it herself. Rather, as in the statement above, she speaks instead of *rewriting*. As usual, Lynn is careful in her choice of words. Lynn's operational definition of rewriting seems to be the act of "correcting" errors in the accidents of discourse—spelling, punctuation, titling, and the like. Such essences as organization of the whole and tone are, seemingly, left undisturbed. There is only a superficial, a surface realignment or correcting the trivial.

Lynn does not voluntarily reformulate because, simply and understandably, she equates reformulation with "punishment work." Also, she does not reformulate because her teachers do not "inspire" her to. What does this word mean coming from a girl who does not seem to ask for inspiration from any other teaching she experiences? She seems to mean first that her teachers, on the whole, write evaluative comments that do not deal with what she is really trying to say; and that they are not really interested in reading and evaluating any reformulation she might attempt. She is in effect accusing them of oversimplification (the equation of reformulating with the "correction" of trivia); and casualness, if not cynicism, in evaluation (they demand correction of trivia, but they will not read and reevaluate a serious effort to recast essences).

Influence of Teachers

The influence of her teachers upon these three pieces of Lynn's writing can, of course, only be inferred. A major source of the investigator's information about the teaching of writing Lynn has experienced is what Lynn says she remembers about such teaching. Also, with Lynn, the investigator is fortunate in having a subject who saved some of her writing from fourth grade forward, including a folder from her tenth grade English class which contained the total output of her assigned writing for that year. The investigator, then, has had an opportunity to see Lynn's composition work for a full school year with all written emendations and evaluations made by her teacher for that year.

One way of approaching the matter of influence is to note what Lynn worries about as she writes; then, to try to find possible origins for her worries in previous school experiences she describes. As she composes aloud, Lynn's energies seem divided between dealing with the actual stuff of discourse and with the amenities. During the writing sessions, she deals explicitly five times with amenities: three concern spelling; one, legibility; one, titling. Once she asks how to spell a word, *terpsichordean*: "Is it 'terps *e*' or '*i*'?" When the investigator does not respond, she spells it correctly with an *i*. Once she asks whether or not she should hyphenate a compound adjective. When the investigator says, "If you wish," Lynn does hyphenate *yellow-and-orange*. In the three pieces of writing Lynn misspells only one word; and she knows it is misspelled: "I forgot how to spell 'questionnaire.'" (Lynn spells it with one *n*.)

Lynn's handwriting is always legible. That she strives for legibility is evident from this comment about an insertion: "Now where can I write that so that it can be legible?"

Lynn, then, is very aware of the amenities of writing, particularly spelling and handwriting. Was she trained to be aware of these? Lynn's first memory of writing in school is that "it seemed to me going through my notebooks from grammar school that all we did was spelling. I had pages on pages of spelling exercises, and really didn't do too much writing at all." The first "theme" she remembers writing is "a composition about ah . . . something about some poor child who never got anything for Christmas and they got a musical teddy bear and they were very happy." She remembers writing the story on the board; in relating the incident she pauses, then breaks off her account with a rather abrupt "That's about all I can remember from third or fourth grade." But later in the session she remembers more, much more: she remembers what made the composition of the musical teddy bear so painfully memorable that it stayed in the forefront of her consciousness for eleven years while all other writing experiences of the same period dropped away:

> I remember writing this composition about the musical teddy bear on the board; our district superintendent was coming in that day and I, my teacher thought it was very good and I spelled *musical* wrong, and she was very embarrassed, that's why I remember the composition, just because of that incident.

Lynn makes five other comments about spelling while presenting her writing autobiography. Her own point of view about her teachers' stress, or obsession, is summed up in one sentence: "They seem to have this thing about spelling."

There are powerful reasons from her past school experiences for her wanting to write legibly, too. For a full school year she was punished for not writing Palmer style:

> In sixth grade I remember we had a teacher who'd give us two grades on a composition, this I thought was horrible, one on composition, and another on your handwriting, and this counted as much, I used to get "E's" on my composition, "E" for excellent, and "F-plus" on my handwriting because it tended to be rather ornate, I had all these little curlicues attached on it, and I have it here, it's really a riot when I look at it now.

The whole matter of "technical correctness," as Lynn aptly calls it, has loomed large not only in her life but in her friends' lives. In fact, she attributes her selection as subject in my investigation to her department chairman's preoccupation with correctness:

> This one girl was in my class, and we had another—I don't know what you could call these courses, you could call them orthodox classes where we just were corrected practically on technical errors, she was getting "B's" again instead of "A's" although I thought her writing was much better than most of the kids in our class. That's possibly why I was picked for this program, this girl . . . could have done it as well but the teacher who . . . liked all these technically correct papers and that's what I turned in so, that's why she liked me.

A last amenity Lynn has clearly been taught: that every piece of writing, no matter what its length or significance, must have a title. Her last act with all three pieces of writing is to supply, reluctantly, a title. "Now, title, 'terpsichordean' means to dance, you could say 'Terpsichordean Greetings' but I don't like it so much." [She writes it at the top of the page] "Is it 'terps *e*' or '*i*'?"

For her first piece the following exchange occurs:

> L: Do I have to title it?
> I: Whatever you wish.
> L: I could get something . . . on 'Profiles of Courage' and make it 'Profiles,' 'Profiles and Smiles,' or something like that. [As she writes it down], Why not?

With her usual self-awareness, Lynn knows she is hostile toward giving themes titles yet conditioned since grammar school toward using them:

> I could never think of an ending, and also the title, this principal of our grammar school had gotten this idea that she didn't want kids writing compositions like my trip to the zoo, and title it like that, so we would write, say, about our trip to the zoo, and maybe it would turn out that we would write only about a polar bear we saw, so the title of the composition would be ahm . . . something about the ice-cream-colored bear, you know, or we would, would get rather imaginative titles, hence when I got into high school I didn't want to put titles on my compositions, you saw last week I really didn't want to put a title on it.

The principal's concern seems to be with the limitation of subject, but note for Lynn the stress becomes one of titling.

Along with one "thing" about spelling, and another about titling, Lynn's teachers also seem to have "this business" about length. Within the forty-five minutes Lynn spends recounting her writing auto-biography, she alludes nine times to the length of pieces of writing, with eight of these related to teacher directives. Again, it is the third-grade teacher, Lynn's first teacher of writing, who first gives Lynn limitations in length:

> So she had us writing, we were limited, in about third grade we were limited to about fifty words.

But other elementary teachers also ask her to observe comparable limitation:

> All through grammar school we were still limited to this, sixty-word business.

In her writing sessions with the investigator, Lynn makes many comments that reveal her concern with length; it is as if she has spent her writing life in school learning to respond only to Madison Avenue contests of twenty-five-words-or-less.

It is not surprising that one of the peripheral skills Lynn has developed in the course of her schooling is the ability to judge, with high accuracy, the number of words comprising any given segment of discourse. "I really don't think I need any sort of a tie-in right here because I'm definitely talking about the manager even though I have this business of about twenty-five words about Burns and Allen." It is probably not accidental, either, that her two prose pieces are almost identical in length, with 289 words in one and 279 words in the other.

Finally, the investigator's policy of nonintervention as Lynn writes makes her anxious, and angry, only once. She asks, "Now how long should this be?" When the investigator doesn't immediately answer her question, she asks:

> Which would you rather see, or aren't you going to say anything, you're just going to sit there nodding your head?

One can only conclude that some of Lynn's preoccupations as she writes have been conditioned by teachers who clearly had as their motto: "The good student writer is the polite student writer."

Lynn worries about elements, as well as amenities, of discourse. She alludes to three "problems" (her words) in her writing—one lexical, one lexical-syntactic, and one rhetorical. First, she is extremely concerned with avoiding the trite expression—what she calls a "cliché phrase." Examples are "striking resemblance," "one of those people who has found his place," and "one of the last things." (She notes no "cliché phrases" in her poem, although an adult evaluator might.) She does not always decide to eliminate these from writing. Although she changes "striking resemblance" to "plain resemblance" (really, a semantic shift), she decides to retain "who has found his place" because it fits into the conversational style she has set for her piece ("the composition is written sort of in a telling manner"); and "one of the last things" because "[it's] sort of a cliché phrase but it's okay."

Along with worrying about triteness, Lynn worries about being "flowery" or "corny"—both terms synonyms, apparently, for pretentious or sentimental. She makes fewer allusions to this stylistic hazard, however. She does decide against using "anticipations were dispelled" with the comment, "I'm always afraid of being too corny because there are some kids in my class who write [like that]."

She repeatedly demonstrates she is attuned to words—their appropriate idiom and their connotative aura: "some word like 'premonition,' only without those fearful overtones"; "'dispelled' sounds as though you had a number of things which are scattered"; "something about 'entrance,' but 'entrance' isn't good because that's like entering school"; and "now a look that is threatening. What's that called?" Lynn never finds "sneer," the word she is probably seeking; and she finally compromises with "stare" (note the allophonic nearness to "sneer").

Lynn also demonstrates an awareness of the relations of ordinates and their enclosing superordinates, a phase of what might be regarded as the logic of language. For example, she changes *picked Snoopy up* to *embraced Snoopy* because "she had to pick him up to embrace him."

Conclusion

Lynn seems to write with greater ease in the extensive than in the reflexive mode. There seem to be both personal and curricular reasons. Personally, she seems a girl reserved about her feelings, although open, even volatile, about ideas. It could even be said she reveals a certain fear of feeling. Also, the curriculum she has experienced in composition, both in elementary and in secondary school, has provided her with very few school-sponsored opportunities for engaging in reflexive writing, as her writing autobiography and a review of her theme folders confirm.

Lynn's view of the composing process is that it is essentially and centrally the act of the first discursive writing. For this inquiry, at least, she devotes very little time to prewriting, projecting, and reformulating activities, while her energy and concentration upon the task of composing aloud are great.

Although the assigning of causality is especially hazardous in matters of teaching and learning, Lynn seems susceptible to the teaching of composition she has experienced. Her view of what portion of the composing process is most important matches the views of her teachers who do not provide school time for the earlier, and later, portions. She worries about what her teachers have stressed, especially the accidents of spelling, handwriting, and length. She tries, often with great skill, to translate directives of high abstractness into sets of behaviors she can enact.

At the same time, there is the inescapable impression that Lynn is more sophisticated than her teachers, both as to the level of her stylistic concerns and to the accuracy and profundity of her analysis of herself as a writer.

CHAPTER 5

SEVEN OTHER TWELFTH-GRADE WRITERS

In this chapter the case studies of the seven other twelfth-grade writers in the sample are compared with the case study of Lynn, set forth in chapter 4, and with one another. The purpose of this comparison is to ascertain if there are shared, or unique, dimensions to the process of composing engaged in by these eight students. The hypotheses set forth in the Introduction will be examined against these comparative data.

Context

As Table 2 indicates, the twelfth graders in the sample do not come

Table 2

Selected Characteristics of the Secondary Schools Attended by the Eight Students in the Sample

	School Attended by					
	Lynn and John	Helen and Rick	Steph-anie	Debbie	Brad-ford	Vic-toria
Size	2200	1650	4785	1600	615	1400
Percentage Racial Distribution:						
White	84	99	85	92	83	4
Black	16	1	14	8	15	95
Oriental	0	0	1	0	2	1
Percentage Attending College	55	75	75	30	98	35
Percentage Dropping Out	12	2	10	35	0	25

Note: The names used to designate the seven students other than Lynn are pseudonyms.

from communities or schools with shared sociological characteristics. However, the schools are markedly similar in the curriculum proffered in English, not only in composition but also in literature and in language.

Family

Although the students do not come from communities and schools with shared sociological characteristics, there are marked likenesses in certain formal characteristics of their families. All but one of the eight is the oldest child in his family; and in that eighth case the student is ten years younger than her single sibling, thus probably qualifying in terms of the nature and quantity of verbal interaction with adults as an only child. According to students of language development, the status of being the only or the oldest child is the most propitious for optimal language development.[1] (Query: is there a high correlation between teachers' choices of "good" writers and those writers' positions in their family constellation? The question might be an interesting one to pursue: perhaps the data most readily available for examination are the kinds of information the National Council of Teachers of English maintains concerning the nominees for the NCTE Achievement Awards.) All remember being read to frequently by parents, grandparents, and other adult relatives. According to their writing autobiographies, at least three of the eight learned to read before they began kindergarten: it is important to recall here that four of the sixteen parents, or twenty-five percent, are teachers. With perhaps the exception of Debbie, the family profiles that emerge from these students' autobiographies compare closely with those found by Dolores Durkin in her extensive study of children who read early:

> What is much more important [than the socio-economic status of a family], the research data indicated, is the presence of parents who spend time with their children, who read to them, who answer their questions and their requests for help, and who demonstrate in their own lives that reading is a rich source of relaxation, information, and contentment.[2]

Given the traditional time-lag between the initial teaching of reading and of composing, it is not surprising that most of the students do not recall writing or dictating stories before they entered school. Bradford does, however:

I: Do you remember when you first wrote stories?

B: Yes I do, in fact. My mother started me out young when I was four. We wrote two stories together and it was kind of funny; it was based on experiences. We used to go out in the park and just look around at nature and things which is kind of funny in a big city but at that time there were a lot of squirrels and birds around they are now and one day we went out in the park and we ran across a squirrel who had no tail. And this was a funny thing to us because how many times have you ever seen a squirrel, I mean, he only had a little stub of a tail so we went back and wrote a little story about it and it was really funny. My mother drew little pictures; it took up about two or three sheets, we wrote it on typing paper, I believe.*

Interveners and Interventions

Parent-teachers are clearly important initiators or interveners for the writing of students in the sample, especially when the students were very young writers. There are allusions in six of the seven other accounts of parents' participation in school-sponsored writing, although, like Lynn, most of the students do not seem aware of the role their parents play, or do not acknowledge it.

Lynn says scornfully about the winner of the essay contest for which she wrote the speech "The St. Lawrence Seaway":

We had to write our speeches and give them before a panel of teachers, and then they picked the representatives from the school, I remember I was very upset that I didn't get to go, they picked some cute little girl who gave some really stupid speech it sounded like the mother wrote.

Yet a few moments later, she says about her own speech:

There are corrections by my mother in it which would be, what I would write the, those are in pencil over the pen so you can still ro-, read what I wrote.

By the time the students enter secondary school, the role of parents in school-sponsored writing greatly diminishes. John seems the only one of the eight for whom a parent-teacher stays a significant other, and even he strictly circumscribes the role his father-teacher can play with an attitude of "Please, Father, I'd rather do it myself."

John notes that peers play no role in his writing life:

J: If I did [need advice] I would probably go to my father first who is an English teacher but if my father were a construction engineer or

---

* Unless otherwise noted, the quotations in this chapter come from the students' writing autobiographies or from the transcripts of their writing sessions.

> something I would probably ask friends for advice but I haven't
> found the need to.
>
> I: Do you read your papers to your father often?
>
> J: Ah, if it's an important paper I'll ask him for some corrections, otherwise I don't because I like to be able to do it myself unless it's a very important paper and still I've written the thing, it's just minor corrections I want and if he starts to give me major ones I just say no and I tear up the paper and start all over again because I like to write it myself.

Two related generalizations seem valid about the role peers play in the writing life of the eight students in the sample. (1) No student in the sample has experienced a curriculum or a set of school-sponsored experiences in composition in which peer interactions play any formal part as, say, in reciprocal reading and evaluating of themes by pairs or groups. (2) Peers play a very significant role in self-sponsored writing of the twelfth graders in this sample.

All five girls refer to a friend or friends with whom they talk regularly about and share their writing—some in an extra-curricular activity, such as the publishing of a yearbook or a literary magazine; others solely and simply as personal friendships.

Significant others among peers tend to be of the same sex, although two of the girls, Lynn and Stephanie, mention boys as well as girls among their writing friends. For Bradford and Debbie, for example, the peer is of the same sex:

> B: There was one fellow at my old school who was a basketball player and he wrote a great deal on his own but it was entirely for his own benefit, he didn't try and get it published or anything. And he carried around a little assignment notebook in his hip pocket and when he felt like it he would write. And he shared it with me; it was kind of an intimacy.

The most extended and explicit case of peer influence is, clearly, the role Paulette plays in the writing life of Debbie—in fact, Paulette is the subject for the second of Debbie's three pieces:

> What amazed me was that Paulette was so serious about her writing. I, too, wanted to write, but gave up easily. Paulette encouraged me to write more often and to put my ideas down whenever I thought of them. Just talking to her about writing helped me greatly.

Only for Victoria, the Chinese-American in the sample, are her writing friends of the opposite sex. Her view is harsh of the girl writers she knows:

I don't really care for my girl friends that write because the stuff they write is just obnoxious.

Two boys are her writing friends:

> One of them is ah, very interested in science fiction, and he's very, he's got a very creative mind, and um, every time I listen to him, he makes me sound so inferior you see soah, so when I go home I get these brainstorming ideas about writing stories, and ahm . . . This other friend—he's, he's, he's really a good friend of mine and he, he writes too, only he's . . . I don't know how really to describe his writing . . . but, ahm, he's got a good influence on me I'd say, but we always discuss what we write about and we, we always discuss other things that make good material for short stories.

In the cases of Victoria and Debbie, certain peers seem actually to provide a role model—that is, the peers see themselves already as embryo professional writers. Both their seriousness of intent and their already-initiated practice of their craft combine to encourage these two girls to emulate their attitudes and their behaviors.

Who the significant other in the composing process of secondary students is seems dependent upon whether the writing is school-sponsored or self-sponsored. For early self-sponsored and school-sponsored writing, when the subjects are preschool or in the elementary grades, parents and teachers seem to be equally significant others. For school-sponsored writing in the secondary school, teachers are the most significant others, with parents occupying a very minor role except, occasionally, when they themselves are teachers. For self-sponsored writing among adolescent writers, particularly the able ones, the significant others are peers who also write.

Nature of Stimulus and Prewriting

Four of the eight students had available for the investigator's use folders containing all writing assigned during the eleventh grade by their teachers of English. A survey of these folders, and the writing autobiographies, reveals that two students wrote sixteen themes for that year; one, fifteen; and one, eleven. Of the fifty-eight themes, forty-one derived from the same field of discourse—namely, they are literature-based—with the tenor formal and impersonal.

Pieces of literature read in school seemed to provide the students in the sample with three sorts of stimuli for writing: (1) a specific style to imitate; (2) a generic style to imitate; and (3) an incitement for an original excursion.

John, for example, recognizes that his style responded "unconsciously" to his reading in his eleventh grade American literature course:

> I: Whom did your writing sound like?
> J: Um, let's see—Wolfe, Melville, Crane.

There was also one conscious effort at imitation:

> J: For a while I consciously tried to imitate Hemingway because I liked his short sentences, but I couldn't do it because I guess I'm no Hemingway, but that's the only author [I imitated].

Victoria responds to meeting a new genre: reading "The Rape of the Lock" in her tenth-grade survey of English literature seems to have introduced her to satire, a mode of writing she finds very congenial:

> V: Oh, let's see. I got a kick out of Pope, Alexander Pope and "The Rape of the Lock." That is what really started me on this writing; this, this, this is the way to poke back at people. . . . It was really funny, how you can really blow up a situation like that, like uhm stealing away of the lock, the cutting away of Belinda's lock, that was funny.

She subsequently writes four satires, two for open school assignments, two in self-sponsored writing. The two school satires are "Beowulf Gets a Program Change" and "Why Revere Took That Ride"; the two self-sponsored pieces are a satire on bad breath commercials, featuring two dragons, "Egbert" and "Belinda"; and a satire of a friend's teacher:

> V: I, I wrote another satire for one of my friends, for on her English class there was this ah . . . male English teacher who'd just gotten out of De Paul . . . and he . . . he wasn't a very creative teacher and he always used to, he loved to hear his voice I mean ah he just liked to read and read.

Victoria astutely realizes the usefulness of satire to a girl who feels exceptionally hostile to adults, particularly teachers and administrators:

> I: Are there any other reasons you think that you wrote, you enjoy writing satire?
> V: Well, you can't really when you get angry with a situ-, when you get disgusted with something, you can't really come up to that person or that organization and say, 'Boy, you really disgust me.' You have to do it kind of subtly, and, ah, so I write these things: it's ah, it's kind of a release of feelings and tension, but yet you don't really hurt anybody.

For Bradford, a teacher's reading of Ransom's "Blue Girls," coupled with the sight of flowers on the investigator's desk, leads to his own exploration of the theme of beauty as his response to the first writing for this inquiry:

> B: Well I was inspired by a poem my English teacher read to us in class about beauties known as "Blue Girls." And the poem was commenting on the fact that beauty should be enjoyed while it lasts and it fades very easily and is very brilliant. So upon looking at the flowers on the desk [the investigator's] I just said to myself that is as good a topic to write about as any other.

Of the remaining seventeen school-sponsored assignments, only three required from the students a response in the reflexive mode: the rest concerned extensive—one might say abstruse—subjects such as cigarette smoking and cancer, the voting age, and the Vietnam War.

Perhaps because they are accustomed to abstract subjects, it is not surprising that for the first two writing assignments in this inquiry, the subjects write six abstract themes (the themes, in the extensive mode, concern capital punishment, the career of engineering, the John F. Kennedy assassination, rent control, Poland, and an experiment in a physics class). It is significant that the three boys in the sample write all but one of the abstract themes. Bradford, the black student in the sample, is the only one of the three boys who chooses to write reflexively (his feelings as he walks by Lake Michigan) and to write poems (he writes two); the other boys write only within one field of discourse, upon subjects that can receive not only an extensive, but impersonal, treatment. Rick refuses to write any response when asked to write a poem or story ("I just couldn't think of anything I wanted to say as a poem or a story"); and John writes a piece of obscenity ("Here; I doubt if this is what you want, but it's what I wanted to write"). If Lynn seems fearful of expressing feelings, Rick and John seem far more fearful.

Their responses are not only all written within the same mode; they are all written within the same species of that mode. The species is that curious one indigenous to the American secondary school classroom—the three-, five-, or seven-paragraph theme.[3] These themes, no matter their length in paragraphs, all have three segments: an introduction of one or two sentences; one to three paragraphs of development with flat, unequivocal "topic sentences" and development by one of three techniques—expansion, comparison and contrast, or example; and a concluding paragraph which is, with a possible change of a word or phrase, identical with the introduction. It is as if the two boys—and Bradford with them when he writes prose—are so thoroughly programmed to a single species of extensive writing that they can readily and comfortably compose no other. The sensation is not unlike asking two unsophisticated computers to compose, then discuss, three themes each.

When asked about their self-sponsored writing, the two boys admit they do not write on their own, except for autobiographies and statements of career plans required by several college application forms. The four girls, on the other hand, write both inquiry-sponsored and self-sponsored writing, within all fields of discourse, with five themes in some way about themselves, and three about others—a Chinese grandmother, a friend, and the people on the Chicago subway. All of them write either a short story or a poem as response to the third stimulus.

What can be the explanations for these striking differences between the boys and girls in their accessibility to invitations in a range of fields of discourse, and in both major modes of student writing? One explanation—and one not wholly satisfactory—is that as a woman, the investigator reminds the boys too much of all the teachers of composition they have had in high school (not one had ever had a male teacher of English!); and they are not rejecting the stimulus so much as the giver of the "assignments." The second is also cultural: perhaps the white boys genuinely believe writing poems and stories is an unmanly activity. Bradford, in contrast, seems perfectly comfortable writing his poetry.

Planning

Bradford is the only one of the eight students in the sample, according to their accounts, who makes outlines voluntarily; he is the only one, too, who makes an outline for any piece of writing produced for this study.

The comments of the other six correspond with those made by Lynn in the previous chapter; the following three are representative:

I: But you ah made no other written plans other than what you indicated here [three phrases in the margin]?

R: That's right. I erased a lot, maybe.

I: How do you go about planning a paper?

J: I don't really get the main idea and then start to write. I start to write and just wherever I end up, I end up. . . . Once I tried to write with a plan and I found it was impossible so I can't see why

> some people say "write out on scratch paper some outline on what you are going to do." I just couldn't do it myself.

As usual, Victoria is the most vehement of the group:

> And another thing I think is that I don't, if you have an exceptional group of kids, I don't think that you should tell them to, to write an outline. I, in my sophomore year this teacher, she made us write an outline, she made us write a rough draft, she made us copy that over, and then hand in the final, and you had to show the corrections. You had to show you followed the outline, that you couldn't have written the story and then wrote the outline. She says she can tell; I don't know; but I used to write the stories and write the outline and she never said anything about it. . . . Teachers that always tell you have to write an outline for this, because it's really a waste of work for the student, if he can write a good essay without having to use all that stuff.

Bradford, on the other hand, apparently outlines for every piece of writing he does. He learned outlining from an eleventh grade teacher for whom he expresses intense and lengthy admiration: "Also I learned outlines, second draft, first draft, this type of thing."

For the first session Bradford decides that "the fact that beauty should be enjoyed while it lasts and it fades very easily and is very brilliant" is "as good a topic to write about as any other." As a first written act he writes five sentences about beauty that will serve as the "five main sections" for the organization of his paper.

As he writes, he observes the outline he initially made:

> Now I am trying to keep to my outline after what I have just written and my next topic was commenting on the rarity of beauty.

and

> Next I have been looking at my outline and as to what I said about the waste of mankind.

Bradford, however, as the accounts of the other seven reveal, is an exception. Despite, or even allowing for his practice, the evidence from this inquiry suggests the following generalizations about planning and projecting:

1. Able student writers voluntarily do little or no written prefiguring, such as written outlines, for school prose pieces of 500 or fewer words.
2. Student writers do no written prefiguring for poems or any other form of private writing.
3. If able student writers are queried immediately before they begin writing, they will reveal that most of the elements that will appear in the piece are present at that period.

Starting

With one exception, the subjects all begin to compose quite as mat-ter-of-factly as Lynn. The exception is Bradford, who tries to start writing, then breaks off in some confusion:

> B: I'm sorry, I don't know what's wrong, I guess the tape recorder just makes me nervous.

When the investigator offers to leave the room and let him practice, he accepts the suggestion with an obvious sense of relief. Within fif-teen minutes, he calls her back from an outer office; says he is ready to begin; and goes forward, composing aloud, without experiencing any more noticeable discomfiture. When they do not block entirely, twelfth-grade writers simply sit down and write, no matter how unusual or unique the setting or circumstances.

Composing Aloud

The general statements made about how Lynn composes obtain as well for the other students in the sample. The first is that their dealings with smaller segments of discourse like the sentence and their dealings with a total piece of writing resemble one another. Both, obviously, in-volve the selection and arrangement of elements—lexical, syntactic, imagaic. Less obviously, there are in the parts as in the whole the same discernible portions of projecting, formulating, and reformulating.

Second, there seem to be certain stylistic principles operating to affect, even govern, their choices of transforms. Indeed, they seem to follow some sort of "program" of style, a program whose origins can be partially traced. This program affects not only their dealings with syntax, but with lexis, rhetoric, and imagery as well.

Finally, the composing does not occur as a left-to-right, solid, unin-terrupted activity with an even pace. Rather, there are recursive, as well as anticipatory, features; and there are interstices, pauses involv-ing hesitation phenomena of various lengths and sorts that give their composing aloud a certain—perhaps a characteristic—tempo.

Like Lynn, other student writers in the sample can be seen trans-lating abstract directives from their teachers into specific dealings with lexical, syntactic, and rhetorical options. Debbie, for example, can be seen attempting to enact her eleventh-grade teacher's directives (they seem not to have been issued as a series) to be direct, concise, and specific.

At the beginning of the third paragraph of the first theme written for this inquiry, Debbie attempts to describe the advantages of running a store "with articles made only by kids." She moves from *This could be learned* to *One immediately thinks of what could be learned* to *Much could be learned*—at once the most accurate and succinct of the three formulations.

Her effort to be specific can be seen in her effort to eliminate vague words like "thing" from her writings. She pauses seven seconds at one point in her sketch of Paulette, then says, "Now I'm trying to think of a word to replace 'thing' again."

Hesitation and Tempo of Composing

Six of the seven other students exhibit the same alternations of actual composing behaviors and of hesitation phenomena as Lynn and with comparable ranges of permutations. There is, however, one startling exception: John's composing aloud consists solely and solidly of actual composing behaviors with no hesitation phenomena intervening. Also, he writes the piece simultaneously with speaking it. He produces 184 words of sustained discourse within seven minutes, at the slow, steady pace of 26+ words per minute. This discourse consists of lexical, syntactic, and rhetorical features of marked sophistication (for example, the first three sentences all begin with the ironic use of the introductory prepositional phrase, *In California*). He makes only eight changes in lexis and syntax, and these extremely minor ones that do not change the piece in any substantive respect.

How can one account for this performance? One explanation would seem to be that he has memorized, and is just recalling for the occasion, a previously written piece; but John states that this is not the case. A second is that he is so familiar with his subject that the actual formulation in writing is a very easy task. In any event, how he writes this piece must remain the most extraordinary aspect of this inquiry, if not its chief mystery.

With the exception of John, the seven other student writers employ the same kind of hesitation phenomena while they compose aloud as Lynn does. As with her, also, there is no pattern to when scribal activity occurs in relation to composing aloud; and there are many unfilled pauses, of lengths from three to thirty-one seconds. Perhaps the most interesting recurrence of a silent behavior is that three of the other subjects, like Lynn, also regularly pause and reread at the end of a unit of discourse they designate a paragraph.

The same kinds of filler sounds occur—[ɜ]; [m]; and "Let's see" and "How can I word that?" The same sorts of self-critical comments occur: "I always mess up my transitions"; and "My dialogue is really terrible." Lynn is more open in her verbal expressions of both pleasure and pain related to her composing; but at least four of the others give nonverbal indications that they are pleased or displeased with the choice of a given option, by facial expressions such as smiles or *moues,* or by gestures.

Lynn shows by far the most awareness of, and interest in, her readers; the others, except for Debbie who seems eager to please the investigator as a reader, seem quite indifferent. Lynn also engages in by far the most digressions, particularly of the ego-enhancing variety. The explanation why could range from speculating she is the most- or the least-assured of the eight. Finally, although other subjects repeat elements, Lynn is unique in the sheer number of repetitions she commits as she jogs in place.

Reformulating

The role reformulations play in the writing process of the seven other students in the sample can be categorized into their definitions, their statements of attitude, and their actual practices.

At least four of the students have a multi-level definition of, and approach to reformulating. For Rick, the lower level is "proofreading— seeing if I left anything out or anything." He does not always "proofread":

> Some other times I don't even proofread. I guess that's not a very good habit either, because I just allow somebody else to read it and correct it because by the time I finish a paper I'm so tired of what I've written that I don't really want to see again until I have to.

The higher level is "revising": "sometimes I actually move things around, but not too often."

For Debbie, there are the same two levels, "proofreading" and "rearranging":

> First I reread, to see if I left out any commas or used the wrong tense . . . . I know a lot of times I don't see better ways to write things and then sometimes I will; I will rearrange a lot.

For Victoria, these levels are "correcting" and "revising": the amount of time she is given or takes for this portion of the process determines which she will do (this also seems true for the others):

It depends upon how pressed I am for time 'cause if I'm pressed for time like the period before I just write the paper, and if it's spelled wrong or something or I've got a comma . . . , I just scratch it out. But if I do have the time and if I really feel good and ready to do it, I'll really make some big changes.

Since in self-sponsored writing the press of time is not a factor, she and the others seem to spend more time reworking in major ways their pieces of writing:

I: Did you do much revising [of the story "The Rice Bowl"]?
V: A lot. I couldn't leave it, leave it alone. I kept coming back and fussing. There's still things I'd like to change, and it's two years later.

Although these students define reformulating and describe the kinds they engage in for self-sponsored and school-sponsored writing, like Lynn, they engage in no reformulating of pieces produced for this inquiry.

Stopping and Contemplating Product

As with Lynn, for all seven other subjects in the sample, stopping, like starting, is a mundane moment devoid of any emotion but indifference and the mildest of satisfactions that a task is over. All end with phrases like "Well, that's it"; "Do you want me to proofread or don't you care?"; "I guess that does it"; "Well, here it is."

Also, as with Lynn, there is no discernible moment or portion of the composing process devoted to the contemplation of the finished product, as in accounts of established writers and artists of all kinds. As there was no comment on beginning, there is no sense of consummation in ending. It is not accidental that eight students, who have adequate lexicons for almost every other phase of full and varied lives, including a critical vocabulary for discussing their own writing, have no *aesthetic* vocabulary, no words to express joy or satisfaction in completion. Or, if they do, they do not regard their own writings as artistic work enough to elicit these words. For inquiry-sponsored, like school-sponsored, writing, they are dutiful enough to want to please—minimally; no more.

Teaching Experienced

Although the students come from eight different elementary schools, their memories of how they were "taught" writing at that level are, strikingly, almost identical. None remembers doing much imaginative writing, such as stories or plays. Rather, there were other emphases:

> In grammar school about all they were interested in was grammar and spelling.

> There was no emphasis on writing creatively. We were working on things such as spelling and grammar.

> We wrote some book reports, I remember. The rest was just grammar and spelling.

> And, um, in second grade we had to write stories for ah, our spelling words; we had about ten spelling words, and you had to make up a story about them . . . . I remember the next story I forgot all about the spelling words and, and I wrote a story, so she took off, well, she gave me an *E* for the story but my spelling grade was terrible.

John sums up the feeling of the group:

> I: How did you feel about this kind of teaching of composition?
> J: Ah, I didn't feel anything until I saw a contrast between high school teaching and grammar [*sic*] teaching. Then I felt that the grammar schools could have done a little better if they had tried.

When asked to describe an ideal, or even a good, teacher of high school composition, imaginations fail: it is as if actual teachers are such inexorable givens, one cannot project beyond them. The most innovative notion is Debbie's who suggests that the use of an opaque projector may help focus students' attention on a given theme while a teacher criticizes it for the entire class.

They can criticize the existing, however. All who have experienced split grading into any polarities—organization/handwriting; substance/spelling; content/mechanics—recommend the use of a single enclosing grade (a universe where there are no grades but perhaps only comments or conferences seems inconceivable; at least, no one mentions it). They banish outlining and correcting of themes "to return on Friday." They also banish lay-readers: "How can she grade us when she's never even met us?"; "Look at this: she wrote all over my letters to Keats and Shelley; the least she could do is write in the margins if her handwriting wasn't so big and shaky."

They share Lynn's worries as they write, although no one else seems so length-obsessed. They wonder aloud how to spell a word; they worry that subsequent sentences do not "develop" a topic sentence; they worry that their introduction and conclusion in the three-, five-, seven-paragraph theme do not match.

The most unmistakable instance of direct response to teacher stimulus is Debbie's worry as she composes aloud about selecting the appropriate tense. In her eleventh-grade folder among twelve themes all of which received an *A* or a *B* is a character sketch of one of Debbie's two younger sisters. Below the grade of *C—*, Debbie's eleventh-grade teacher writes:

> By using the present tense this becomes an analysis rather than a sketch. You're telling about what you *know* to the reader. It's your analysis of Debbie.

At no time does any of the students ask aloud any variants of the questions: "Is this subject important to me?" "Do I care about writing about it?"

CHAPTER 6

FINDINGS

The following summary of the findings of this inquiry is based upon the behaviors and reports of the eight students in the sample.

General Findings

Twelfth graders in this sample engage in two modes of composing—reflexive and extensive—characterized by processes of different lengths with different clustering of components. For the twelfth graders in this sample extensive writing occurs chiefly as a school-sponsored activity. Reflexive writing is a longer process with more elements and components than writing in the extensive mode.

Reflexive writing has a far longer prewriting period; starting, stopping, and contemplating the product are more discernible moments; and reformulation occurs more frequently. Reflexive writing occurs often as poetry; the engagement with the field of discourse is at once committed and exploratory. The self is the chief audience—or, occasionally, a trusted peer.

Extensive writing occurs chiefly as prose; the attitude toward the field of discourse is often detached and reportorial. Adult others, notably teachers, are the chief audience for extensive writing.

Components of the Composing Process

Context. The context for a given process of composing supplies the interveners and interventions into that writing process. Who are the significant others from the environment depends upon whether the writing is self-sponsored or school-sponsored. For self-sponsored writing the most significant other is a peer. For school-sponsored writing, the most significant other is a teacher.

More specifically, who the significant other in the composing process of secondary students is seems dependent upon whether the writing is school-sponsored or self-sponsored. For early self-sponsored and school-sponsored writing, when the subjects are preschool age or in

91

elementary grades, parents and teachers seem fairly equally significant others. For school-sponsored writing in the secondary school, teachers are the most significant others, with parents occupying a very minor role except, occasionally, when they themselves are teachers. For self-sponsored writing among adolescent writers, particularly the able ones, the significant others are peers who also write.

Nature of stimuli. In school-sponsored writing stimuli are most often pieces of literature being studied in class or abstract topics, such as the draft, drug addiction, and the ABM missile system. In self-sponsored writing the students interact with a wider range of stimuli from all fields of discourse. In self-sponsored writing they often write about "self" and "human relations."

Prewriting and planning. As noted under general findings, prewriting is a far longer process in self-sponsored writing; indeed, in school-sponsored writing, there is often no time provided for this portion of the composing process.

Able student writers voluntarily do little or no formal written prefiguring, such as a formal outline, for pieces of school-sponsored writing of five hundred or fewer words. For self-sponsored writing, especially the writing of poetry, the students in the sample do no written prefiguring. This is not to say that these students do not operate from a plan, at least in extensive writing; when questioned immediately before writing, all, or almost all, features and components of their discourse seem present.

Starting. The students in the sample start school-sponsored writing, or writing in the extensive mode, very matter-of-factly with no displays of blocking or temperament. Not all students—in this sample boys, notably—can accept invitations to write in the reflexive mode and exhibit rejecting or blocking behaviors when confronted with such a stimulus.

Composing aloud. Composing aloud is a specialized form of verbal behavior characterized by the alternation of actual composing behaviors and of certain specifiable kinds of hesitation phenomena.

The most common hesitation phenomena are making filler sounds; making critical comments; expressing feelings and attitudes, toward the self as writer, to the reader; engaging in digressions, either ego-enhancing or discourse-related; and repeating elements. Even the student writer's silence can be categorized: the silence can be filled with sheer scribal activity or with reading; or the silence can be, seemingly, "unfilled"—"seemingly" because the writer may at these times be engaged in very important nonexternalized thinking and composing.

In the composing processes of twelfth-grade writers an implied or an explicit set of stylistic principles governs the selection and arrangement of options—lexical, syntactic, rhetorical, imagaic. Often the source of such a set of stylistic principles is an abstract teacher directive which the student tries to translate into behavioral terms and apply through his process of composing.

Stopping. Although stopping is a discernible moment in writers' accounts of the composing process, it is not one in school-sponsored writing of students in this sample. For self-sponsored writing, however —notably, poetry—the students experience such a moment, like the famous "click" Yeats describes upon completing a poem.

Contemplating the product. For school-sponsored writing students do not pause to contemplate what they have written. For self-sponsored writing there occasionally seems to be a pause for such contemplation.

Reformulation. Students do not voluntarily revise school-sponsored writing; they more readily revise self-sponsored writing.

Seeming influence on writing by teachers of composition. The first teachers of composition—by giving certain descriptions of the composing process and by evaluating the products of student writing by highly selective criteria—set rigid parameters to students' writing behaviors in school-sponsored writing that the students find difficult to make more supple.

These descriptions of the composing process differ markedly from descriptions by established writers and with the students' own accounts, conceptualizations, and practices. Students' awareness of these discrepancies leads to certain behaviors and attitudes: outward conformity but inward cynicism and hostility.

Most of the criteria by which students' school-sponsored writing is evaluated concerns the accidents rather than the essences of discourse —that is, spelling, punctuation, penmanship, and length rather than thematic development, rhetorical and syntactic sophistication, and fulfillment of intent.

CHAPTER 7

IMPLICATIONS

Implications for Research

So much remains unexamined about the composing process of children, youth, and adults that this chapter could well become the longest in this study if a full catalogue of such research questions were attempted. Consequently, only those pertaining in some direct way to this study—subjects, correlations, data-collecting techniques—will be presented here.

First, if the size of the sample of twelfth graders were enlarged, generalizations about the composing process of this chronological age group would be more valid. A sample could also include twelfth graders of a range of verbal abilities, with fairly equal distribution of high, average, and low abilities.

As in studies of linguistic performance, such as those conducted by Hunt and O'Donnell, students of different chronological and ability age groups could be examined, using a design similar to the one employed in this study and employing the same, or similar, writing stimuli.[1] Again, as with Hunt, twelfth-grade processes and practices could be compared and contrasted in systematic ways with adults, both with those known to be skilled in writing, such as professional writers, and with an average population (Hunt, for example, in his current studies, uses firemen as representatives of an average population with only a high school education).[2]

Another interesting approach would be to make longitudinal case studies of a given sample of students, following them from the time they begin to write in the earliest elementary grades throughout their school careers, up to and including graduate school. Such an approach would permit far more direct observations by investigators of how writing is taught, and learned, with little reliance upon the memories of the subjects and upon indirect evidence of the teaching of composition experienced. More important, it would make better known the developmental dimensions of the writing process, both for the individual and for members of various chronological and ability age groups.

Possible inter-relationships could be ascertained between the findings about the composing process of a given group of students and their scores on certain standardized personality and creativity tests such as the Thurstone Primary Abilities Test, Minnesota Multiphasic Personality Inventory (MMPI), Thematic Apperception Test (TAT), Rorschach Test, Torrance Minnesota Tests of Creative Thinking, Getzels-Jackson Battery on Creativity and Intelligence, and Myers-Briggs Type Indicator.

Perhaps responses to the following questions could be obtained: Do high creatives follow a composing process that is telescoped or transmogrified when compared with the composing process of, say, students with high IQ's or students with low creative ability? Is there a correlation between general personality traits and preference in modes of writing? Is there a correlation between a certain personality and a certain composing process profile: for example, is there a high positive correlation between ego strength and persistence in revising?

Cross-cultural studies of how students compose could be made both intra- and internationally, perhaps with certain variables or dimensions singled out for scrutiny. For example, if members of certain cultures have little interest in, or concept of, the future, as with the Arab or the Hopi, will they engage in any of the kinds of prefigurings for writing found in Western culture, such as prewriting and planning?

Perhaps the most promising aspect of this study for further research and model construction is the characterization of the behaviors involved in composing aloud. There are indications in this study that certain findings concerning transforming operations and spontaneous speech also obtain for composing aloud; particularly applicable are studies of Frieda Goldman-Eisler and George A. Miller, discussed before in chapter 4 (page 67). As noted there, what seems to be required for more accurate information is a study with a finer calibration than this one, and one, possibly, employing cross-checking techniques and mechanisms to assure reliability in the data. Possible techniques include (1) the use of time-lapse photography and (2) the use of an electric pen or stylus whereby a record can be kept of every time a student starts and stops writing.*

---

*A camera arrangement whereby the subject would record his page or piece of writing every time he made a change or an addition (by pressing a foot-shuttle-shutter) was suggested to the investigator by Richard Braddock, one of the authors of *Research in Written Composition*. At first consideration, the camera seems far more intrusive than a sympathetic investigator sitting by and making notes; the pressing of a foot-shuttle-shutter more artificial than talking aloud;

Implications for Teaching

This inquiry strongly suggests that, for a number of reasons, school-sponsored writing experienced by older American secondary students is a limited, and limiting, experience. The teaching of composition at this level is essentially unimodal, with only extensive writing given sanction in many schools. Almost by definition, this mode is other-directed—in fact it is other-centered. The concern is with sending a message, a communication out into the world for the edification, the enlightenment, and ultimately the evaluation of another. Too often, the other is a teacher, interested chiefly in a product he can criticize rather than in a process he can help initiate through imagination and sustain through empathy and support.

A species of extensive writing that recurs so frequently in student accounts that it deserves special mention is the *five-paragraph theme,* consisting of one paragraph of introduction ("tell what you are going to say"), three of expansion and example ("say it"), and one of conclusion ("tell what you have said"). This mode is so indigenously American that it might be called the Fifty-Star Theme. In fact, the reader might imagine behind this and the next three paragraphs Kate Smith singing "God Bless America" or the piccolo obligato from "The Stars and Stripes Forever."

Why is the Fifty-Star Theme so tightly lodged in the American composition curriculum? The reason teachers often give is that this essentially redundant form, devoid, or duplicating, of content in at least two of its five parts, exists outside their classrooms, and in very high places—notably, freshman English classes; "business"; and in the "best practices" of the "best writers"—that, in other words, this theme somehow fulfills requirements somewhere in the real world.

This fantasy is easy to disprove. If one takes a constellation of writers who current critical judgment would agree are among the best American writers of the sixties—Norman Mailer, Truman Capote, Philip Roth, Saul Bellow; and their juniors, Gloria Steinem and Tom Wolfe—where, even in their earliest extensive writings, can one find a single example of any variation of the Fifty-Star Theme?

As to freshman English classes, the assumption is that freshman

---

while the time-lapse technique of photography still requires the examiner to infer the intervening portions of the composing process.

A member of the Physics Department of the University of London had begun developing an electric pen for the use of the research team of Britton, Rosen, and Martin, according to a conversation the investigator held with Harold Rosen in July, 1968.

English is a monolith, rather than a hydra-headed monster with perhaps as many curricula and syllabi as there are harassed section men and graduate assistants. In "business," where can one write the Fifty Star Theme except as a letter to an unheeding computer or as a Pentagon memorandum?

The absence of match between what is being taught secondary—and, undoubtedly, elementary—students and the practices of the best current writers is partially attributable to teacher illiteracy: how many of the teachers described in this inquiry, would one guess, have read one or more of the writers mentioned above? Yet without such reading of wholly contemporary writers, teachers have no viable sources of criteria for teaching writing in the seventies, even in the single mode they purport to teach. No wonder that many of the students who are better- and newer-read reject models that are as old as exemplars in the secretary guides of the late eighteenth century and as divorced from the best literature of their time. (This is not to say that the only models should be works of the late twentieth century; great works from all centuries are contemporary, as the writings of Donne, Swift, Coleridge, and Carroll will attest.)

More crucial, many teachers of composition, at least below the college level, themselves do not write. They have no recent, direct experience of a process they purport to present to others. One reason may be that there are in the United States very few teacher-training institutions which have intensive and frequent composing as an organic part of the curriculum for young and for experienced teachers of English. In England, such programs seem more common, as do experiences in allied arts through creative arts workshops.[3] When, if ever, have our secondary school teachers painted, sung, or sculpted under any academic auspices?*

Partially because they have no direct experience of composing, teachers of English err in important ways. They underconceptualize and oversimplify the process of composing. Planning degenerates into outlining; reformulating becomes the correction of minor infelicities.

They truncate the process of composing. From the accounts of the twelfth-grade writers in this sample one can see that in self-sponsored writing, students engage in prewriting activities that last as long as two years. In most American high schools, there are no sponsored pre-

---

*Exceptions are the NDEA Summer Institutes at the University of Chicago I directed and codirected the summers of 1965, '66, and '68; and the 1969 EPDA Summer Institute at Northwestern University, directed by Wallace Douglas.

writing activities: there is no time provided, and no place where a student can ever be alone, although all accounts of writers tell us a condition of solitude is requisite for certain kinds of encounters with words and concepts. (If teachers assume that the student will find elsewhere the solitude the school does not provide, let them visit the houses and apartments in which their students live.)

At the other end of the process, revision is lost, not only because it is too narrowly defined but because, again, no time is provided for any major reformulation or reconceptualization. Despite the introduction of modular scheduling in a few schools, a Carnegie-unit set toward writing, and the other arts, still prevails.

Much of the teaching of composition in American high schools is probably too abstract for the average and below-average students. This inquiry has shown that some able students can translate an abstract directive such as "Be concise" into a set of behaviors involving the selection of lexical, syntactic, and rhetorical options. But there is no indication they were taught how to make such a translation in schools. There is also no indication that less able students can do such translating on their own—at least, without constant and specific guidance by their teachers.

Much of the teaching of composition in American high schools is essentially a neurotic activity. There is little evidence, for example, that the persistent pointing out of specific errors in student themes leads to the elimination of these errors, yet teachers expend much of their energy in this futile and unrewarding exercise. Another index of neurosis is the systematic confusion of accidents and essences (one wonders, at times, if this confusion does not characterize American high schools in general). Even the student who, because of the health of his private writing life, stays somewhat whole is enervated by worries over peripherals—spelling, punctuation, length. In *The Secret Places,* as elsewhere in his writing, David Holbrook describes these emphases:

> Children become so terrified of putting down a word misspelt, particularly an unfamiliar word, that they don't put down any words. I have seen it happen to a child of 8, who wrote long marvellous stories. After a year with a teacher who wrote 'Please be more tidy', 'Your spelling is awful', 'Sloppy'—and never a good word, she stopped altogether. She wrote little lies, a sentence at a time, in a 'diary'. 'Coming to school today I saw an elephant.' It wasn't true. But that was all she was damnwell going to write—neat, complete, grammatical, well-spelt, short, and essentially illiterate lies. For her the word had been divorced from experience. The deeper effect is to make the learning process one separated

from sympathy, and a creative collaborative interest in exploring the wonder of being.[4]

What is needed for a reversal of the current situation? Assuredly, frequent, inescapable opportunities for composing for all teachers of writing especially in reflexive writing, such as diaries and journals. For teachers at all levels, given the mysterious nature of learning and teaching, surely some value will adhere to having their own experiences shaped into words for pondering, perhaps into meaning and illumination.

Perhaps their students will gain benefits as well, as the result of such teacher training. Perhaps teachers will abandon the unimodal approach to writing and show far greater generosity in the width of writing invitations they extend to all students. One wonders at times if the shying away from reflexive writing is not an unconscious effort to keep the "average" and "less able" student from the kind of writing he can do best and, often, far better than the "able," since there is so marvelous a democracy in the distribution of feeling and of imagination.

Finally, a shift may consequently come in who evaluates whom, and to what end. In this inquiry we have seen that the most significant others in the private, and often the school-sponsored, writing of twelfth graders are peers, despite the overwhelming opportunity for domination teachers hold through their governance of all formal evaluation. American high schools and colleges must seriously and immediately consider that the teacher-centered presentation of composition, like the teacher-centered presentation of almost every other segment of a curriculum, is pedagogically, developmentally, and politically an anachronism.

APPENDIXES

APPENDIX A

Writing Autobiography

Lynn, Second Session

Lynn: When you called this morning I was sitting in the middle of my base-ment floor with a lap full of old notebooks from sixth grade and I just jumped up and they flew all over.

Investigator: The first thing I wanted to ask you this morning is to ah, try to describe to me if you've thought about the topic I mentioned to you last time, and sort of how and when and under what circumstances and, as pre-cisely as you can recall.

Lynn: Well the . . . the topic being . . . you mean the autobiography sort of thing, because you said something about, something else . . . well . . . it seemed to me going through my notebooks from grammar school that all we did was spelling, I had pages upon pages of spelling exercises, and really didn't do too much writing at all. I, I have a couple of . . . things here that I did do, one of them being a poem which I don't remember whether I wrote or whether we copied out of our spelling books but, it looks like something bad enough that I probably wrote it [See poem, "A Spooky Time," p. 104.] ah . . . we didn't, in our grammar school our principal had been an English teacher, she taught at H—— High School for a while, so she decided when she came in and I was in third grade, which is just about when we start writing, to develop this new thing so we don't just get compositions like ah, 'I went to the museum with my mommy and daddy. We had fun,' and call it *The Museum* or something like that . . . So she had us writing, we were limited, in about third grade we were limited to about fifty words, which is a lot for a third grader . . . and . . . I remember writing compositions, they we- they were very short . . . and they were mostly, about school, or . . . about people that I knew, I really can't remember, and I don't have any examples of a real composition that I did. I can remember things . . . oh yes I do, now I remember. I remember something about a musical teddy bear, and . . . it was about, it was a composition about ah . . . something about some poor child who never got anything for Christmas and they got a musical teddy bear, and they were very happy . . . oh I was the musical teddy bear in it that's right. Now I remember. I don't remember exactly how the composition was worded, but I remember writing it on the board and I was the musical teddy bear and, so-and-so the kid whoever it was, was very happy to get me and I played some song I don't remember what it was . . . that's about all I can remember from about third or fourth grade . . . and, I skipped half of fourth grade and, half of fifth grade, and looking over my compositions, from the end of fifth grade, I never seem to do very well on them, like I'd always be getting G's and, you know, well you know I had

Rm.107 Gr.3 B

October 6, 1959

A Spooky Time

October's the time to set the date,

When we'll be trick or treating late,

The spookiest costumes you've ever seen,

Will be worn by us on Halloween

to get E's all the time you understand (laughing) and, I think I might have an example of one, here, I don't remember. Now this is sixth grade, I have an awful lot of stuff from sixth grade, but nothing from the fifth that I can find . . . oh, in fourth grade . . . oh I used to, explain things like, I used to have a, not explain but I used to have a lot of I think, and by this I mean, in fourth grade there's a composition here . . . I have 'When the teachers had their Christmas party we too had fun.' By this I mean we watched them from the sidewalk. We saw party hats bobbing by the windows, and tried to identify the wearers by their hair color. We had as much fun as the teachers, I think.' [See p. 105] Now the "I think" is sort of a bad way to end a composition. This was written, as an exercise in an English workbook and we had to write about, something we did on a holiday . . . Now, the construction . . . I know, it's not so much you know like, "I did this and I did that," the first sentence I think is rather complex for, you know like a fourth grader, "When the teachers had their Christmas party we too had fun." Now I don't think I talked like this at this time . . . I still don't. My writing has always tended to be more formal . . . than my speech . . . let's see . . . in sixth grade and all through grammar school we were still limited to this, sixty word business, and we would write book reports four sentences long.

When the teachers had their Christmas party, we, too, had fun. By this I mean we watched from the sidewalk. We saw party hats bobbing by the window, and tried to identify the wearers by their hair color. We had as much fun as the teachers, I think.

Investigator: Was there any explanation given you on this?
Lynn: Because it, we tend, when grammar school children are told to write a hundred fifty words they tend to ramble, and they don't put much (clears throat) pardon me, many pertinent things in. Now one thing that they liked us to do is on book reports, I remember we did an awful lot of them, I think I have one or two with me, we, most kids would write, "I read *Jane Addams* by Augusta Stephens" or something, "it was about a girl." Well they had us writing book reports of the style, I think I may have one here, about ahm . . . you'd give a little bit of the story like . . . the one I think I have although I can't find it right now is . . . let's see, it was about two Egyptian kids I just read it this morning, it's something about ahm, so-and-so and so-and-so, 'Dick and Jane' I don't remember the names . . . 'crept through the dark hall underneath pi-', no 'crept through the passageway into the pharaoh's tomb. They had heard that, a robber had gotten into the place and decided on their own to investigate because their father the keeper of the tomb would have been in trouble. As they rounded the corner, a blade fell from the ceiling. To find out what happened next, read.' [See "Social Studies Book Report," p. 106.] We used to do a lot of book reports like that . . . The compositions really weren't that fantastic, like we used, half of the compositions we did was write something using dialogue, because that was what it said in our English book, and since we were limited to, about fifty words, nothing much ever came of it . . . It's funny that ah . . . a lot of the things that I read I can see reflect . . . my . . . you know, my ideas at that time. Having skipped this, one composition I think you know was in fifth grade, I was behind most of the kids athletically, I could never keep up with them in gym, and I wrote a composition with dialogue, with a Sue, which obviously was me, talking to Marilyn, who was one of my friends at the time, talking about a, volleyball game or sa-, or some kick baseball game or, baseball game and I said, I was saying in the composition, the dialogue was very stilted, I, people don't talk like that, it was something about, 'that was a very good catch you made ji-,' I was talking to Marilyn, 'you know you, it really was good because you let Lynette score,' Lynette being another girl we knew, and Marilyn says, this is the close for

Room 203 GRADE 6A
JUNE 9, 1962
Social Studies: Book Report

Would you like to read an adventure, two mysteries, and two love stories all wrapped up in one thrilling tale? If so, the book *Three Golden Nobles* by Christine Price is for you! It is the story of a young serf named Stephen who meets Gilbert, a young painter. He decides to run away to London to become a painter. A young girl, Marian, helps him to escape. When he gets to London he presents a letter of introduction, given to him by Gilbert, to Master Thomas Lovecok, a master painter. In a while he becomes an apprentice and meets another apprentice named Harry and the two become fast friends. Then up pops a mystery involving Phillip, a journeyman who works for Master Thomas. Back at the manor Marian and

the composition, she says 'yeah, but you won the game for us.' There's no explanation of what I did, but this is the sort of thing I would have liked someone to say to me . . . Now . . . maybe it was, the influence of my teachers or something, I have no idea but, the language, or maybe it's just that all kids write, formal language, when they're having dialogue it's not very . . . natural at all . . . oh, now this is, an interesting thing I did in sixth grade, I just found this, this morning I'd forgotten about it, there was a *the peasants are having trouble with Roger Baliff who is in temporary charge of the Three Manors while Sir Richard, the handsome young lord of the manor, who is in love with Marian, is away at war. Well anyway, Sir Richard finally comes back and everyone (except wicked Roger) turns out happy in the end.*

I enjoyed this book very much because the plot kept me captivated all the way through. This book will be of eta interest to almost anyone because of the many different things covered in this book. (For example; if you are interested in crafts during the Middle Ages you may like the discription of Master Lovecok's shop.)

speech contest sponsored by I don't know who, it might have been the school system, this is when the St. Lawrence Seaway opened, this is, the, thing was dated March 1962 . . . and, they picked two kids from every seven, sixth, seventh and eighth grade class in the school, to participate in a speech contest and, we had to write our speeches and give them before a panel of teachers, and then they picked the representatives from the school, I remember I was very upset that I didn't get to go, they picked some cute little girl who gave some really stupid speech it sounded like the mother wrote . . . Now, this was the first, long piece of writing I think I probably ever did, not counting science reports which . . . usually composed of, I have a couple of them here . . . a couple of, like a page on, say forced air heating and then a page on, radiation heating, but they were not extended pieces of writing (See, for example, "History of Refrigeration," p. 108) . . . [The one on the Seaway] looks like it's about, I don't, two hundred words which is a lot . . . for me in sixth grade, and I really don't think, I could write a much better one now. There are corrections by my mother in it which

History of Refrigeration

The main purpose which refrigeration serves is to keep food fresh. Man, after hunting, often had a surplus of food. In warmer regions this meat was usually smoked to keep it from spoiling. In the Arctic regions, however, man soon learned that the cold would keep his meat in good condition.

In warmer regions cold was also used to preserve food. This was done by digging cellars next to the source of a spring. The running water on the stones of the walls cooled the food.

The Chinese, as far back as 1000 B.C., got ice from the mountains, packed it in sawdust or sand, and used it for preserving food in a crude sort of ice box.

Clipper ships carried ice to southern regions of our country because our American colonists also used methods of refrigeration.

would be, what I would write the, those are in pencil over the pen so you can still ro-, read what I wrote . . . My sentences tended to be rather choppy, but . . . it seems to be fairly well organized, would you like me to read part of it or something, I can read the whole thing:

'When Chicago became an inland seaport with the completion of the St. Lawrence Seaway, one of the greatest changes in the city's trade history occurred.' Now I had 'When Chicago became an inland seaport after the St.

Lawrence Seaway was completed,' my mother changed it around it sounds more grown up, this is the only time I think she's ever, corrected anything I wrote, 'Chicago has always been a center of trade,' that's how I started. My mother changed it, "Visible even to Joliet and Marquette wu-, was the value of this sight as a place of trade,' now, my mother changed it to 'From the time of Joliet and Marquette the value of this site as a place for trade was recognized' . . . then I have, 'here b- two branches of a river flowed into the lake, the Southern branch giving access to the Mississippi by waterway and a short portage for entry, to the fertile Illinois country. Since Chicago is the only city on the St. Lawrence Seaway that has direct water connections with the great Mississippi Basin, it has both unusual opportunity and respon-sibility . . . The five ports in the metropolitan area handle over forty per cent of all import and export general cargo, that is loaded and discharged at the American Great Lakes ports, so . . . ' that's a mouthful. I had 'there are five ports in the metropolitan area, at the present time the seaport of Chicago handles' . . . my mother was just I think, changing it to get longer sentences so I didn't have those short-, short choppy things . . . 'Chicago's already established position as a railroad center makes it convenient for the imported goods to be shipped into the city by rail, after the manufactured products are ready for sale the railroad again ships them to market. Chicago's switch district takes care of eleven per cent of the nation's freight car loading. It handles about thirty thousand freight cars a day. There are nineteen trunk line railroads and the combined mileage of these is about half that of all the railroad systems in the country. Chicago leads the nation with transportation in the air too.' I had 'as well as on the ground.' 'The title nation's busiest air-port has passed from Midway Airport to O'Hare International, Airport, O'Hare Field.' That wa-, that's very awkward . . . 'with its ek-, with its facili-ties for jet air traffic and the most modern air passenger accommodations in the country. If a success of the international trade fair, held . . . annually since four years ago acts as a barometer, I think Chicago's future in the world of trade is bright.' [See reproduction of speech, pp. 110-11] Now, that was a rather technical report in parts, and I think they wanted us to do something like um . . . This will give us an opportunity to meet people from many lands, or something like that, I think I could have done a better job, ah, it would have been more creative had I first written about, our going to visit the ships that were coming in at Calumet Harbor, our family went, visited a French ship, an Israeli ship and a German ship . . . that probably would have been more interesting than all this technical, business but . . . can't say much about that now. In, in the seventh grade we had this, En-glish teacher who we thought was crazy, he, I think he's, got his Ph.D. you know and he's teaching at Loyola or something like that, he, struck me as being rather frustrated. One day . . . he used to give us all these short things, like capsule, things like, our eighth grade English teacher had us do, thirty second impromptus like, we'd get up in the front of the room and she'd say, you will now speak for thirty seconds or a minute on whatever it was on the subject of, shoelaces, and the person would have to speak on shoelaces. Now what Mr. T———— did was, we were sitting in the auditorium one day with nothing to do we had his first study, it wasn't our real class, he said, write twenty-five words on any object in the auditorium. Now since it was an old school there were a couple of interesting things, there were huge cracks in the wall and, ah, a couple of odd looking pictures . . . I wrote about the . . . pedal on the piano, and I wrote how, Mr. T———— who our, all the girls in our class were in love with him because he was the only young male teacher in the entire school, he said, Jump practically, on the pedal and I put how it was all, ah it was getting banged up after, the teacher whose place he took had been, there she played the piano so gently, kept banging the thing, and, I don't, I don't have that composition I was, I found part of the scratch copy but I think it was . . . changed entirely from what I have, oh yeah . . . I, this was the beginning, of a composition about the piano itself and then I narrowed it since I only had twenty-five words . . . to . . . the pedal, at the bottom . . . I had something in the composition about how many teachers must

ROOM 203 GRADE 6A
MARCH 21, 1962

[SPEECH]

When Chicago became an inland seaport, with completion of the after the St. Lawrence Seaway was completed, one of the greatest changes in the city's trade history occured.

Chicago has always been a center of trade. Visible even from the time to Joliet and Father Marquette was the value of his site as a place of trade. was recognizing Here two branches of a river flowing into the lake, the southern branch giving access to the Mississippi by waterway, and a short postage for entry to the fertile Illinois country.

Since Chicago is the only city on the St. Lawrence Seaway that has direct water connection with the great Mississippi basin, it has both unusual opportunity and responsibility. There are the five ports in the metropolitan area. At the present time The Seaport of Chicago handled over 40% of all import and export general cargo that is loaded and discharged at the American Great Lakes ports. Chicago's already established position as a _railroad center makes it convenient for the imported goods to be shipped to the ~~to other parts of the country~~_

S. W. & n.

Raw goods are shipped ~~into~~ the city by rail ~~and~~ After the manufacture of products are ready for sale the railroad again ships them to market. Chicago's switch district takes care of 11% of the nations freight car loading. It handles about 30 thousand freight cars a day. There are nineteen trunk-line railroads, and the combined mileage of these is about half that of all the railroad systems in the country. Chicago leads the nation in transportation in the air as well as on the ground.

The title "~~The~~ Nation's Busiest Airport" has passed from Midway Airport to O'Hare International Airport (~~O'Hare Field~~) which has excellent facilities for jet air traffic and the most modern air-passenger accommodations in the country. ~~If the super~~ the International Trade Fair held annually since four years ago acts as a barometer in the world of trade.

I think Chicago's future is indeed bright.

have played it because the piano looked like it was about sixty years old . . . Another interesting thing we did is, this guy also taught art, we had him for about two different, two or three different classes, he drew a picture of a beer mug with this thing sitting in it that looks like a Dr. Seuss character with a, mortar board on its head, I can't show it to the tape recorder but . . . se- and he had us write a brief yarn, he said, about it . . . and I wrote about how, this guy had a pencil mug on his desk so, I embellished the picture by drawing pencils in the mug, and I wrote about how it scared him one day by appearing in a puff of smoke. We were encouraged in that class to use our imaginations which we never got in any other class, it seemed . . . we kept writing things about um, what I did this summer or what I did over Christmas vacation, spelling exercises, put all the spelling words about thirty of them into a fifty-word composition (laughing) we would get some really weird things from those . . . and, also for this, teacher . . . we wrote, we adapted a story . . . that we had, into play form . . . now I think I did this whole thing in two days, in other words like I left it to the last minute, no I did the last, two scenes or acts or whatever they were in about two days I can see there are no corrections made in it whatsoever, just was writing straight through . . . The dialo-, I had too much narration, for now it, it might have been, for then, and, I always had my players speaking out loud like, the first scene opens and, if I can find . . . yeah, here's, the kid is sitting on the stage and, you don't, the, the narrator says 'Our play opens at Ye Old Antique Shop we see Chuck Ames sitting behind the counter, Chuck fresh out of high school has just announced to his boss, Mr. Utterback that he was quitting after today.' Chuck says, 'boy, am I glad I'm leaving this, joint or, no am I glad I'm leaving this dreary job' . . . even though, I can't read the scratch copy I'll have to get the other one . . . it's just that Chuck tells you absolutely everything in about five lines of dialogue . . . here it is he says, 'boy, am I glad I'm leaving this dreary job, the pay is good but my work is so dull, just a few people coming in every day to pawn small items, I wonder who those mysterious visitors Mr. Utterback keeps having are?' That was really great, offhand construction there. Chuck goes on to say, 'this shop f- is full of junk, the only valuable thing in the whole place is that tray of semi-precious stones I lock ov-, up every night before I leave.' Now right away you know that this is a mystery, that he's going to forget to lock up the tray of stones . . . I really don't know how, the story had so much detail in it, it was rather hard to adapt to a play, if I had time to work on it now I could probably do a better job, at least I hope I could you know four years later I should be able to do something better . . . the . . . yeah and the boss says 'here are your wages for this week, time to go' I, this is completely unnatural . . . and Chuck later walks in front of a, oh he says ah, 'hm, the man, he's in front of a movie theater, hm, the mannequin's necklace looks pretty good, say that mannequin's wearing the actual jewels used in the film, jewels oh my gosh I forgot to lock up the jewel, tray I must go back.' This wasn't in the story, this was something I put in, and, I think it's the best piece in the whole thing, because that . . . you have ah, the narrator says much too much . . . oh . . . the, bli-, there's a guy who's allegedly blind and, Chuck sneaks back to the shop and, is crouching behind the counter and the blind man opens the door, lights a match and looks in, that was the, Chuck of course says, 'a blind man who lights matches in the dark?' Now I think, I didn't know at this time that an audience could get . . . could, you know understand you know they would, see him, they would recognize the man you could something on him, some recognizable thing like, some, a hat with a very large brim that people had noticed so they'd, you know be sure to remember him . . . now ah . . . he talks too much, I, I think the reason, this play was bad was because, I don't think I'd seen very many plays at that time, I'd probably seen, Goodman Theatre children's productions, and I'd been in, a production of *Oklahoma* at our community center when I was in about fourth grade, but I really didn't know how to write a play and we didn't get much preparation. I think, our teacher just was trying to see what we would do with it. It seems all the teachers I had would give us interesting courses were either doing research or working on their Ph.D.'s and I think they're using all our material . . . this teacher really gave us . . . he would lecture on what the humanities were, stuff like that . . . in high school, the first thing that struck me was we were supposed to write compositions of two hundred words . . . and this was really, a shock to the kids from our school, I don't know I, it impressed me more than anyone else I think, and that we had never had to write anything . . . so . . . long before, we'd been writing these forty-to-sixty-word compositions. In eighth grade we wrote almost nothing. Our English teacher spent most of our time since the staff of the school newspaper was in our class, spent most of our time working with us, on the newspaper, we had no writing, and for an entire year before you hit high school and you get a teacher who expects you to write . . . it, that was very bad preparation. I don't have any of the compositions I started to write in high school, I have them at home I think, or I have the scratch copies. I don't know exactly what drawer in my desk they're in, but I forgot to get them. They were very, they didn't use much imagination, I don't think . . . although I was never very good at writing fantasy, it was just that, writing these things is really a drudge . . . I found that if I could write about a specific incident, and use, specific facts, I was doing a lot better than if I just had to write about like my ambitions . . . I'm sure we had to do a composition on that theme, ah . . . it was very hard, it still is very hard for me to write about abstract things like feelings about something, I do a lot better when I have facts . . . some of the best ur-, the best writing I ever did in high school was my biology term paper, well, I did in my freshman year, and, also, I don't have any of them now but I had a lot of essay tests, in eighth grade, I might have a couple of those at home ah in science classes, like, explain such-and-such, and the writing on those was better than the stuff I was writing for composition classes, it was more organized . . . possibly because I had specific facts to organize . . . and I wasn't just writing about 'we went here' and 'we went there,' I found it much easier to write about those, and my freshman year we had to trace the evolution of, the organism and I did a whole parallel thing about . . . tracing it along with the embryo and, it was really a very good piece of writing if I could find it I'll bring it in, because, you know, it's, it was the first time I think I ever used a parallel construction, where I actually carried something out in a parallel construction, you know comparing something, instead of saying oh like ah, 'as round as a butterball,' like writing about my little sister, (Reproduced on pp. 114-16). In my sophomore year we did a lot of analytical things like I did, a paper on . . . Captain Ahab as Machiavelli's Prince, now I've never read Machiavelli's *Prince* I just based the entire thing . . . or ah maybe I made it a Machiavellian view of Captain Ahab I just based it on, the ends justify the means . . . if someone really wanted to jump on me you know someone who was familiar with the material, they thought, my teacher thought good [See essay reproduced on pp. 118-20.] I had another idea for that same paper on Moby Dick to compare, the witches in Macbeth to Fedallah the, you know, whatever the Indian, the, mystic in this book, and thi-, those are rather adventurous . . . on, Thoreau, we had to write a paper the duty of civil disobedience, I think, I compared, I wrote something about how people . . . were really you know mad at him because here he is he's not paying his taxes because he doesn't believe in the war, I think it was the Mexican War at the time . . . and then I, was writing well done

A—

English A2C Per 1
January 19, 1966

My Views of Deborah

Henry David Thoreau speaks thusly of the partridge chicks in <u>Walden</u>, "The remarkably adult yet innocent expression of their open and serene eyes is very memorable. All intelligence seems reflected in them." Whether one has in mind partridge chicks or infant humans, all young things possess this intelligent innocence. I, as does the rest of my family, seem to forget that my sister Debbie is no longer a baby; but she still has this magic quality of changing chameleon-like from six-year-old brat to Rhodes scholar.

A little 6-yr.-old girl with stick straight, brown hair walks over to the table where I am working on a physics problem. "Susan, what is that white ruler for?"

"It's a slide rule and it multiplys. Isn't it late for you to be up?"

"Noooo!" the little girl stamps her foot then stalls, "How does it work?"

"By sliding the middle stick."

"What's multiply?"

"Multiply is like when you take one number and then take another and another of it."

"I know." (T-affirm on "I")

"What's two two's?"

"Two two's?"

"Two AND two"

"Oh, four!"

"Now put the one on this black
row of numbers over the two on this red
row...

"Gimme it!" the little child stamps
her foot. Ten minutes later she shows
her older brother how.

There is another side, a typical brat
side, to Deborah parteally shown in her
foot-stamping. Debbie just loves having
her own way in everything, whether it
be checkers or keeping the light in the
hall on at night. She claims to "see
things" and will scream until the
light goes on because she realizes
her sisters need sleep and Mom turns
on the light so she will be quiet.
And Deb has won again, which
she must. In any competition Debbie
wants to win and has to win. When she
is pitted against her peers she usually
does win ("Mrs. Feely picked me to be captain
three times.") competing against
betters frustrates her.

The development of Debbie's own character
will take a long time, more so because
she is the baby if not a baby. When
she plays the piano she screams when

her brother David calls her "Deberace
Liberace."
　"Barbara, what are you going to be?" to
9-year-old Barb.
　"A horse and dog doctor."
　"Me, too."

　"Debbie, you play it with a black
key," my comment.
　"Nooo!"

　"Debbie, help David set the table," is a
request from Mom.
　"Unh-unh."
　"Deb-bie, please."
　"Unh-unh."

　These are a few of the Deborah's
I know, the others are yet to be born.
　"Susan, why are you writing about
me?"
　"Because you're fascinating."
　"What's 'fasanating'?"

Children, because they haven't
accomplished much, are of limited interest.
You certainly do all you can with them
subject. The details are well-chosen and
intelligently organized.

about the usual thing about well, Thomas Jefferson went and broke laws and, things like that, but, we got more interesting aspects, most of the things we wrote in this course were . . . with relation to the books we were reading or we'd have to write something copying someone's style . . . There was something in the back of my mind about writing, a two hundred word, we had to write a two hundred word paragraph of description, of something. I don't remember what it was, and I don't remember what I was describing . . . this last year as I said, in the last session we did hardly any writing at all. I think that my writing has, actually, going down since my sophomore year when we had to do all these, projects and stuff . . . that's about all I can, think of, for writing style.

Investigator: Let me ask a few questions if I may
Lynn: Sure
Investigator: about, some of the things that you were saying, ah, and pick up certain details
Lynn: O.K.
Investigator: Um, one of the firs-, one of the, first things you were saying, and you were talking about very early grades like, third grade, now you said something about you had ah, scratch paper, ah does this mean you ah did some kind of planning before you wrote your themes?
Lynn: Oh . . . in, no, that wasn't for third grade, that was for about . . . fifth or sixth . . . I, think that, we would be given, a topic say, before recess, she'd just say you're going to write after, ah, this afternoon or something, so you'd sort of be thinking about it . . . during the lunch . . . I remember writing a composi-, we had to write something about fire drills in second grade that, that was right after coming back, well that was sort of a disciplinary paper, why we should be quiet during a fire drill, but . . . I don't really think we did much planning, what we would do, this ah, this I remember now, is in third grade we would write out our compositions on a piece of paper, then put them on the board, and the class would criticize them or s-, one person would go up and criticize, this was in third grade I think that was rather sophisticated for third graders, I remember writing this composition about the musical teddy bear on the board, our district superintendent was coming in that day and I, my teacher thought it was very good and I spelled *musical* wrong, and she was very embarrassed, that's why I remember the composition, just because of that incident . . . well we used to, and even in eighth grade we were putting compositions, the lu-, the few writings we did we put on the board . . . in seventh grade, with this one teacher we would get assignments the night before, you know, write a composition on, and hence, we did some planning. What I did . . . in most of mine, is I would try and write the whole thing, straight through, no planning, but I would end up, I'd get past the first two sentences and I'd want to change it, so I usually did . . . I wrote it out, I would write out a composition completely, then I would go through, and while I was writing I would make corrections, then when I copied it over, you know for a good copy, I was still making corrections . . . you could say that I would do, three drafts, because I would write it . . . and then be correcting it as I,

would write it, and then when I copied it over it was different than, what, you could read off of the scratch copy . . . for reports, for, technical things, I've never done outlines for compositions which, might help me, sometimes . . . if in this, course when I was a sophomore, I would write down two or three points and I'd put them in what order, like one two three four and then I'd put two where four was, and things like that . . . I'm really, most of my compositions I read the last twenty-five words, well this was true in my freshman year, I wrote the last twenty-five words at ten to eight before my class, because I could never think of an ending, and also the title, this principal of our grammar school had gotten this idea that she didn't want kids writing compositions like *My Trip to the Zoo*, and title it like that, so we would write, say, about our trip to the zoo, and maybe it would turn out that we would write only about a polar bear we saw, so the title of the composition would be ahm . . . something about *The Ice Cream Colored Bear*, you know or, we would get rather imaginative titles, hence when I

OK—A English A2C, Period,
December 13, 1965

Captain Ahab as
Machiavelli's Prince

OK

In *Readings* in *Political Philosophy*
Francis W. Coker comments on
Machiavelli's great work as follows,
"The Prince treats of the means
whereby a strong and adroit man may
most successfully acquire, increase
and perpetuate political dominion.
Questions of right and wrong, consideration
of public welfare or of conformity to
religious creeds, are introduced only
with regard to their bearing upon
the success of an autocrat."

underline title

It would almost seem that Captain
Ahab, in Herman Melville's Moby
Dick, was a student and practitioner
of Machiavellian philosophy, so closely
do his actions parallel the above
quotation. Captain Ahab was the
autocrat of the microcosmic Pequod.

For him to gain and hold "political
dominion" over his crew as important
to him as to a statesman on land.
The land-bound ruler uses his
control over his subjects for his
gratification in, for example, extending
his territory. Ahab needed the full
power of the Pequod's crew to fulfill
his mission of revenge against
Moby Dick.

Ahab may have been a maniac
but not the "raging" variety. He
reasons carefully and sees clearly
what he must do to accomplish
this "political dominion." In a
duplicate of Adolph Hitler's tactics
he uses mass psychology. Utilization
his dramatic ability and playing
on the ignorance of his mental inferiors
result in the desired end. In Chapter
124, "The Needle," Ahab magically makes
a compass from a sailmaker's needle.

"Abashed glances of servile wonder
were exchanged by the sailors...; with
fascinated eyes they awaited whatever
magic might follow."

This is the kind of (sea) dog like
obedience which Ahab desires and succeed
in obtaining with a Machiavellian
sweep. He pushed aside "right and wrong,"
"public* welfare," "religious creeds"
(*Family?)
only making use of them where
they furthered his means. Where
they interfered with his plans
they were even more harshly
treated. The prime example is
Chapter 132 "The Symphony"
where Ahab finally rejects even

his family in his quest. But this Machiavelli did not caution Ahab against abandoning himself in the quest. (His Machiavelli did not tell him of a greater power which could vanquish his) effective   reputation

You have two good examples of Ahab' use of mass psychology. Your paper would have been even stronger with others — the blood ceremony with the harpoon, the luck with lightning coming from masts and harpoon, & the toast drunk from harpoon heads.

got into high school I didn't want to put titles on my compositions, you saw last week I really didn't want to put a title on it . . . and . . . we . . . ah, I would try and think of a clever title, sometimes they came out rather, cliché like . . . but they weren't you know like *My Trip to the Zoo, My Summer Vacation, My Ambition,* we tried to be more imaginative, it didn't always work . . . but, that's the way it, happened. Planning, I've never really done much, really. I plan it more in my head and then put it down.

Investigator: You mentioned that, just for one composition that your mother ah, made some, revisions ah, prior to your submitting it for the purpose

Lynn: This was the speech

Investigator: Mhm, and you said it was the only occasion that adults, other adults ever ah, work on your writing, before, you submitted it, say to the teacher or to a contest?

Lynn: No, never, I can never think of an incident, sometimes I would have, trouble, phrasing something and I would go downstairs and say to my mother or my father you know, what do you think would be better in this case, I'm looking for a word, but, I never wanted to show them what I wrote, I, I never liked what I wrote, this was particularly true in my freshman year in high school, it seems that I would turn in all these compositions I thought I should get F's on, and the theme reader, we had a theme reader for some of our, she would give me A's on them and, I didn't like them, but, I guess, they thought they were o.k. for a high school freshman, I thought I should be writing a lot better things than that . . . it's interesting to note that, two of my girl friends who are fantastically creative people one who plays five musical instruments, and, she writes, her writing tends to be rather flowery now but, when we were in grammar school and I've known her since, I was very young, her writing I thought was always excellent, she wrote, in our sophomore year an entire, poem, a lyric poem it was about, three typewritten pages it was about, Ahab talking to the whale, about the, all about the whale's eyes, very interesting, and the other girl, has been writing, poems on her own since about fourth grade which is, really, out of the ordinary, well in all these classes where I said I was surprised that I was getting "A's" on my themes, they were getting poor grades . . . perhaps my themes were technically correct in that I built up to a nice climax and that my, spelling was right and my constructions were right, but they were never very imaginative . . . this might be a reflection on the teacher . . . and, in this creative course we had when we were sophomores, one of the girls was in the course the other one wasn't, the girl who was got very good grades . . . and I was getting good grades too, possibly because we were encouraged to use our imagination, but again this year . . . this one girl was in my class, and we had another, I don't know what you could call these courses, you can call them orthodox classes where we just, were corrected practically on, technical errors, she was getting "B's" again instead of "A's" although I thought her, writing was much better than most of the kids in our class. That's possibly why I was picked for this program, this girl Susie could have done it as well but, the teacher who, Mrs. _____, liked all these technically correct papers and that's what I turned in so that's why she liked me . . .

Investigator: You're talking in a way about ah the way teachers evaluate themes, ah I wonder if you'd share with me what you remember about what teachers ah wrote on your themes or what they said about them.

Lynn: Well, in . . . up until high school all they would write would be like 'Very good' or they'd correct spelling and punctuation, they seem to have this thing about spelling . . . In high school, in our freshman year, again we, having, corrections in spelling and punctuation and, never anything about um . . . why don't you use such and, why don't you bring out this instead, or, something like that . . . we would, although last year, it was funny, we would comment that Miss _____, this teacher who we thought was very good, she would write, a commentary that was more, that was longer than your composition, she would say, 'I thought your construction in such-and-such a case was very interesting, but, you might have an even more effective theme if you just limited it to, a comparison of those two, items say,' and so then we'd rewrite the composition as, as she suggested. It seemed to me that all the rewrites we ever did was so, they would be, technically correct, I remember in our freshman year, most of the corrections were technical, and if we had more than three corrections, even if it were three misplaced commas we had to copy the entire theme over . . . and, I was looking at some of my friends' copies and second copies, the graded ones and then the corrected ones and, there's no difference in the writing, I never . . . took it on myself to, rewrite a composition. The only suggestions we ever had were from this teacher last year who really gave us some, constructive ideas . . . ahm . . . that's about it, with due respect to them.

Investigator: Why do you think you chose not to revise?

Lynn: . . . Partly because it seemed to be a punishment work, we were just said, if you have more than so many mistakes, you have to rewrite your composition and it has to be in by the Friday after, and . . . she never would . . . our English teachers never rel-, I mean maybe she talked to me about my compositions I don't remember but, I never remember any suggestions, which inspired me, to rewrite something, so that there was any change in it the, so that it was any better, the only changes seemed to be technical ones . . .

Investigator: You mentioned something about grading and the ah, grade schools about "G's" and "E's", do you remember how themes were graded at other grade levels?

Lynn: Do you mean like

Investigator: Were "A's" and "B's" used or comments?

Lynn: Well they changed the entire grading system of the high schools in, I think it was just before my freshman year and they went on the yearly plan and they stopped having, junior graduation, in grammar school there were four grades, "E," "G," "F," "U" . . . and I was always got "E's," and, you know an occasional "G," and if I got an "F" it was absolutely you know horrible, I could never you know live it down practically, but in high school we were graded A,B,C,D,F . . . in sixth grade I remember we had a teacher, who'd give us two grades on a composition, this I thought was horrible, one on the composition, and another on your handwriting, and this counted as much, I used to get "E's" on my composition and "F-plus" on my handwriting because it, tended to be rather ornate, I had all these little curlicues attached on it, and I have it here, it's really a riot when I look at it now . . . um . . . there was never really any, unorthodox grading, we were never graded on, construction as opposed to content or creativity.

Investigator: Mhm . . . ah, did you notice differences between the way your theme reader graded your themes and your regular teacher?

Lynn: . . . We thought the theme reader was more lenient, and that, some things our teachers would grade we would get lower grades on . . . they graded for the same things though, as I said these girls who were creative and had all these wild compositions, got much lower grades or . . . I don't know their, their theme, they lacked technical correctness . . . occasionally they would say, you know this sounds babyish because you were using all these short choppy sentences, but . . . the teacher that, we've only had a theme grader once, last year, since our teacher only taught our class she had plenty of time to, watch and, this year I don't even count . . . but . . . if we had, oh, I know of one case from another class, where there's a teacher who, I don't know it seems yi- I can separate English teachers in creative ones and orthodox ones, theme graders, from what I've seen tend to be rather orthodox, they grade you mostly on style, not style pardon me on, technical correctness . . . this one teacher in our school whom I'm going to have next year for this creative lit program, sent some of her things to a theme grader because she's very busy and, she doesn't have time to grade them all the time, and she's always disagreeing with the theme grader like, someone might, turn in a theme . . . that, the theme grader will give say a "B" to, and Miss_____ will say, no that's a "C" composition, you showed absolutely no imagination, you've been writing the same thing for weeks . . . and, she will disagree . . . I guess, theme graders tend to be . . .

I don't know they're, retired English teachers (laughs) so, they, they don't know the kids which is different, they don't know that ah, Joe could be writing much better compositions because, he's talking in class shows a much better imagination than what's coming out on the papers . . . that's about all I can say about theme graders, I, haven't had much experience with them.

Investigator: Ah, you were saying that ah, you felt more comfortable, when your writing concerned facts, or the organization of facts, rather than some expression of feelings, why do you think this is so?

Lynn: I really have no idea. This is, this is just something about me. I would rather . . . I'm a great organizer, and I'm going to run into trouble maybe on the yearbook this year, I can, do well in activities, I think maybe I have this whole complex about . . . with the editor before me, he was an extremely able guy, I told you he, entirely changed the yearbook copy to stream-of-consciousness, which is something I've never seen in a yearbook, and I could point out all sorts of, organizational faults, and a couple of faults with relation to, the average, uh, he said the poor slob reader of the book, where they wouldn't understand what's going on at all, like, most of the kids don't even read the copy that, you know some of it was just really far out . . . I've always . . . I've always had trouble talking to people about, my feelings on something. I can quote from other people I can . . . talk about, ahm . . . I can talk about facts more easily than I can talk about abstract things . . . when . . . I was at this institute, one of the kids kept saying, Lynn you know, you're a great kid but you know it doesn't come out in our discussion group because you seem to be talking in clichés, you never seem to be talking about yourself, about your own feelings, you seem to be giving examples all the time, I don't know why this is, I could, get some sort of explanation, rather I'm sure, but I don't know.

Investigator: Do you ever write anything about your feelings when there's not an audience involved say ah, or teacher or sa- or friends?

Lynn: I can only think of two instances, when I have written something; about, because I felt very strongly about something. I have one of them here if you want me to, to read it, this is, from the institute, where we had all this intensive things, I told you last week about how this one social worker got up in the middle of this nice discussion group and started yelling, and also the first line in this, there was a lot of talk about smoking, that is because a lot of the kids smoked, and . . . when we seemed to have a particularly tense discussion group the kids would start smoking so, it started off, 'this is enough to make me start smoking. A woman got up on stage and just about damned us all to hell for sitting and talking and not doing, well what are we supposed to do. I'm frustrated by the helplessness of the entire situation. Here we are ninety teenagers, at least forty-five of whom are very concerned, but we can't help the South Vietnamese mother,' there was, we were singing this song about, Vietnam and there was a picture on the stage, 'but what are we to do, go to Vietnam, march in Chicago, somebody tell me please,' and, this was written, I can't read it, well, but, I mean I could cornball it up but, it was really written under stress, I, there was no one really, to talk to because the kids were just, utterly just walking around you know, my god there was this horrid, and everybody was saying the same things you know, what are we supposed to do we're ninety miles from Chicago out in a camp, there's nothing we can do [See "This is enough . . . ," below] . . . and the whole camp was just in an uproar and, this was one of the only things, the other thing I wrote last week, I was very upset, because I'd gone out with this kid on Saturday night, and we had a real great time, you know, sometimes you go out, most of the time I go out with people I don't really like them, but just you know just to go out practically, my mother thinks I'm a big snot because I'm always laughing at the boys I go, you know, I don't mind if they're kooky, if they have all these crazy, habits, but if they act like they can carry them off it's o.k.

This is enough to make me start smoking!

Norm got up on stage + just about damned us all to Hell for sitting + talking + not doing. Well what are we supposed to do!! I'm frustrated by the helplessness of the entire situation. Here we are 90 teenagers; at least 45 of whom are VERY concerned. But we can't help the Vietmother! What are we to do — go to Viet Nam! March in Chicago! Somebody tell me! Please!

Like one boy I went out with had this, obnoxious straw hat he would wear all the time. Well this other guy you know also wears funny hats, but he, you know he's sure of himself, he doesn't . . . there's something about his entire bearing which makes it, which means he can carry it off as such . . . so I went out with this kid, and we were supposed, it was supposed to be like we were going out in a group only there were six kids, three boys and three girls and, two of the other kids had been dating, in fact the other four kids had all been dating for a while, they'd broken up and stuff like that, and this boy that I went out with I'd known, the girl he was dat-, I'd known him once, he's three years older than I am, but I've known him since I was a freshman in school, cause he was dating a girl who was in BBG and, we were good friends, so she was always talking about, so I knew quite a lot about him, and I hadn't seen him for quite some time . . . and I was just talking to him about all sorts of things, and then we were walking over to get, you know pop or something, and so he takes my hand and this is very romantic and then we went and watched the Grant Park fountain and we really had a nice time, and then, he didn't call me all week, and I was very upset Wednesday, because, this other boy had called me up and asked me out to lunch, and he said that, he sort of hinted about taking me out, this weekend, and I sort of pushed him off because I really wanted to go out with this other kid, and he didn't call me up and I was very upset, and so Wednesday night, I just read about, how, when I knew this kid in high school I was you know like, his girl friend's little sister so to speak and, I'd always been running around and, you know giggling and all, all over the place, and now I seem to have grown up, and I wrote this thing, I tore it up because I didn't want anyone else to see it but, that's the only other time I've written something, about how you know . . . now I hadn't seen him for almost a year . . . and, you know I'd seen him r-, I'd seen him like you know, wave to him, but I hadn't seen him for almost a year, and I seem to have changed a lot in a year . . . and this is what I wrote about and it was all, what a nice time we had and, that was it.

Investigator: Ah, why do you think you wanted to write it down?

Lynn: Because I was extremely upset, and there was nobody I could talk to because . . . one of, I don't know, there's no one, my mother, was very upset, was, not, not she's very upset, she was very busy because one of my little sisters was going out of town the next day and, she had to help her pack, and anyway it was very late at night, I'd come home from work late it was about . . . no I'd, I'd been someplace, it was about eleven o'clock at night and my mother was tired she wanted to go sleep, and my little sister she was asleep already and . . . I don't know, one of my girl friends who I've known for quite some time . . . I could have, called her up and talked to her . . . but, she's a, at some sort of stage now where, she hasn't been dating anyone for about a year, she's gone out once or twice but, I think, she's really what I would call desperate, and so she's not really the person to talk to, it's just that I wrote it down because there was no one to tell it to . . . and I was really, upset, and, I have this one book I don't know whether you've ever read it, *The Prophet* by Kahlil Gibran, and I was reading part of it, and I was really, partly because I may have been overtired but I was really, worked up, I just, I was thinking about it, and I went into my brother's room and got my stationery out of the desk, and I was sitting up on my bed with my little you know high-intensity lamp on my shelf writing this thing, I really wrote it because there was no one to tell it to. I very rarely have such, intense feelings about something . . .

Investigator: M hm, m hm . . . do you read Gibran often?

Lynn: . . . Usually, in this case I decided I wanted to read it because, I mean I think it's such, it's so beautiful, I have another book that I really like which is similar, only it's not reading it's pictures, it's the *Family of Man*, a photographic exhibition. I don't know, one of my girl friends said, she just likes to read it because it makes her feel nice, and there are a couple of things, there was one thing in the book that, was very close to what I was thinking, something about . . . something about . . . I don't remember whether it was about talking or whether it was about love or something like that, I wanted to read what he said about it, to see if, my thoughts were anywhere, close to it. It was something about . . . if in our fear, oh it was about love and, you know how . . . love really exposed, you know like, what you really are and it said something about, if in our fear we are afraid, to, there was some metaphor about threshing, a threshing floor, if we are afraid to you know, if we are afraid of ourselves then we must leave love's threshing floor and go out into the world and laugh and weep, but only weep half our crying and laugh half our laughter, something like that. I read it . . . it started last year at this institute when one of the girls had the book, and I'd never seen it before . . . and then when I got home, I got a belated, present, from this girlfriend of mine I mentioned before was very creative and everything, of this book, and I read it. I was reading parts of it . . . and parts of it really seem, it really seems this guy knows some, you know like he really pinpoints things. A lot of kids, have read *The Prophet* and I know there are a couple of other books, kids that are normally you know like, rah rah sorority or rah rah BBG and they don't, they . . . hate, a couple of people because they're intellectual snobs they say, but they really like, reading the book, I guess . . . everybody finds something in it.

Investigator: M hm . . . Are there other books like it?

Lynn: I've only run across, a couple that I really like. I'm na-, I could look I guess, in fact that's, probably what I'm going to do because I have to put together a wa- a library for the institute this year. So I'll look around for some. I don't know, there must be.

Investigator: M hm . . . let's turn to a, ah turn to a quite different kind of subject, and that is to go back a minute to the kinds of teachers of English you've had. And, I'd like for you to, speculate for a while about, what would be a good teacher of composition.

Lynn: . . . A good teacher of composition

Investigator: M hm

Lynn: . . . I think the teacher that I had last year was, a good teacher of composition because, when she assigned a composition it was never as a punishment assignment, and it wasn't like we have to write one composition a week, which, the kids don't like . . . and also one thing she was very good about, she se-, she would give us a two day, deadline on it like she would say, it's due Friday but if you turned it in Tuesday it was o.k. . . . Most of the kids turned them in on Friday, because, you know we felt that, she's not going to, give us a grade that is not going to be, you know, we can, that we won't be able to get a better, grade on . . . she would, this teacher . . . would make intelligent comments about, our themes like, she liked this one theme that one of the boys in our class did about a sale he did, when he was in third, in, no he must have been about six years old he held an auction. He needed some money he decided so he auctioned off things like comic books. And, the language of, him as the auctioneer was very, it was very professional sounding and she wanted, she wrote a whole thing that she doesn't think any, five year old would ever talk like that, and, a bad teacher of composition would just give the kid, a "C" on the composition or, you know just downgrade it because, because of this, but she gave David a chance to . . . write back to her saying that he'd, seen sa-, a lot of, cartoons or something about auctions and he knew what auctioneers said when he was that age . . . and so then she, said well in that case, you know she gave him a better grade on it and, she seemed to encourage the kids if they would, write out something crazy like that. I think the theme on that one was something about um . . . I don't remember what the theme was, it was something about ambitions.

Investigator: Did she always give you the theme on which to write?

Lynn: No I don't think so, sometimes, once or twice I think she just said write . . .

Investigator: M hm
Lynn: That's always the hardest for me because there are a lot of things I can write on . . .oh, her, she had an overhead projector so, in which, we would . . . have, was it, we practiced writing expository paragraphs all the time, and . . . it was very good, they would have the sentence on it, and she had a grease pencil which she could write on the sides what she would say like, now how do you think, what would be better about this sentence, so a couple of kids would offer suggestions, or she'd put a theme from one of the kids in our class on the overhead projector, we would write up our own corrections on them, and then you know like, when we would go through the theme in the class, we would, you know, go over it, everybody would see if their corrections were what, you know, stylistically consistent, or whether in our corrections we were just rewriting this composition as we would write it, you know trying to force our styles on, the other person. If the teacher can make the kids aware of something like this I think it's great.
Investigator: Do you remember anything about the order in which she did things, what she did, early in the year or in the middle or late?
Lynn: . . . I really don't, I think that, early in the year . . . we had all this business about with the, projectors, and writing, you know, looking at the examples, and then later in the year we did semantics, which I think she started out with, technical things, but they weren't as, dry as things we'd had before, they weren't, English workbooks where we had to ah, put in the periods in the right place, or rewrite twenty-five sentences putting in all the correct capital letters which we'd had for, years and years and years we'd been doing things like that. . . . And then, I don't think we . . . oh yes we did, right in the beginning of the year we had a creative take off session where we had to do something, we'd, were given about three weeks to prepare, a creative, something creative on *The Red Badge of Courage*, one boy did a painting, another kid, sepa-, played flamenco guitar so he, did something like that and then, I was in this little skit, that we did about a mother, whose son has gone off to war . . . and, she started right away with having us use our imaginations while she was giving us all this technical business, it sort of livened it up, later in the year we got more involved like I said I wrote this theme about, *Moby Dick*, which was, rather an ambitious project, I don't think I really should have tackled it at that time, and, we became more aware of styles, we talked more about style and writing as the years went, as the year went on.
Investigator: Ah you mentioned her by name, was it Miss _____?
Lynn: [name given]
Investigator: Yes, I, I know her, would it be all right if I would ah, ask her if she still has, your themes?
Lynn: Oh yeah, I think she does
Investigator: Mhm, m hm
Lynn: Yeah
Investigator: We know of each other because of meetings we go to, and I thought I, ah she's one of the three English supervisors isn't she, yeah
Lynn: Yeah, she had taught at [school] for a while
Investigator: Oh had she, I didn't know that, uh huh

Lynn: And, then she left about, she left I think just before my freshman year, and maybe before I was in eighth grade, and I guess the Board of Education wanted to see what this *English Syntax* would be . . . or how the kids would like it, or maybe this was her own project, I don't know, so she came back, and we had her first class in the morning you know like, and she'd have to be downtown at nine o'clock and our class was over at eight forty, so we were always staying till ten to nine you know and then she'd have to run . . . and she only had our class which was really fantastic because she could really concentrate on what we were doing, she only had one set of papers to grade, and one lesson plan to do up . . . and, that was, it was a very good class, we liked it, possibly because we were spoiled because we had this one teacher who devoted all her time to us.

Investigator: M hm, m hm . . . I have a few more minutes here

Lynn: Yeah

Investigator: (laughs) Just as a reminder for next time ah, the topic would be to write about a person, idea, or event that, especially intrigued you, and would you try to keep a, some kind of informal record of, how you think about it then the next week, or, if you've already thought about it you know, where and when and how, and then share it with me at the beginning of next session

Lynn: Is that such as say, I could talk about taking a bus ride downtown . . . you know, I might be able to get something interested, interesting, I was thinking about this . . . tonight we're going to have a bridge game at my house and I've invited these two boys that I've both been dating and neither knows that the other's going out with me, that should be interesting. Also, I notice all these queer people on the bus going, like today, these two old ladies got on, they were straight out of *Arsenic and Old Lace*, they had, very tall, very spare looking, they must have been in their sixties, their skirts were half way to their ankles, they looked like something out of the 1930's, and, they, I thought they were very interesting, occasionally I see like, I think old people are very interesting, to watch them, and see what they do, little kids too . . . I might be able to get something, just from, some of the people I work with or some of the people who come in to the store I could, take one of them . . . you want it on one thing though, not like

Investigator: One thing

Lynn: Yeah that'll limit it better, one thing last year in our English course she, said 'your writing should be clear concise and memorable,' those were our key words, and, we really tried to make our writing as concise as possible, we would, we were always limiting our topics, I remember starting compositions and then, taking like one paragraph, out of my composition, or one thing I mentioned and then rewriting the entire composition on that one thing . . . cause I wanted to go into it more.

APPENDIX B

"Terpsichordean Greetings"

Lynn, Third Session

Investigator: If you had a chance to think about the assignment theme for today, could you tell me a bit about what kind of contemplation you had on the topic?

Lynn: Well I have, it's interesting I've been thinking about, thinking about it, you said well remember what you think about it so when I think about I have to remember this which is kind of artificial. But I thought of a couple of topics that I could write on and some of them will be interesting but it's hard to find original ways to approach something. This is what I was thinking. I don't want to come up with something trite.

Last week I had said how I noticed how I always think old people on the bus and everything were very interesting. And my grandmother stayed with us for the weekend and it sort of struck me that she was a lot older than she used to be and I thought this might be an interesting topic. I could write about that, it's probably the best of the lot. Then I get preoccupied in personal problems, about these two boys I know lately and I was thinking I could write about one of them but then that wouldn't be too interesting to anyone else. This morning I thought, oh, I was thinking about writing about these people like about this one boy. I could have started like, "Well the first time I went out with him," I could talk about that. I could just see it starting out, "it was just one of those evenings" or something like that which would be just too trite.

I was reading this magazine yesterday, *Seventeen* magazine, which is this fashion thing that everybody reads because it tells you what to wear and things like that and they have all these soppy stories in them and I would not like to turn anything out like that. It might be interesting to write something just to earn money for it but they're not that interesting really, they have a limited audience appeal. This magazine is aimed at high-school-aged girls and those are the only people who'd be interested in this sort of a story.

This morning I had an idea to write about this thing we got from my sister who is on vacation with our cousins. She sent us from, it might have been Disneyland, a two-foot-high cut-out of Snoopy, the Peanuts dog dancing, and my mother set it up in the middle of the living room so you see it when you walk in the front door. And I thought it might be interesting to write about people's reactions to it, there have been quite a few. And I was thinking of, I had two extremes in mind. This one boy when he walked in the door sort of curled up his nose at it, and I could just hear him thinking, "My, how gauche can you get?" (laughs) And one of my girl friends came and she picked up the thing and she said, "Oh, I love Snoopy," and she

Terpsichordean Greetings

One of the last things someone would expect to find in a livingroom with walnut-paneled, book-lined walls would be a very large cardboard statue of Snoopy, the Peanuts dog. But in our livingroom anything is possible. He dances with an expression of utter bliss on his face, his arms held open in greeting directly in the path of anyone entering the front door.

Since he is unavoidable, all visitors to our house must register some sort of reaction. My girlfriend Barbara, who also holds her arms open in greeting to the world, embraced Snoopy in all his cardboard cuddliness and cooed, "Isn't he sweet?" The cardboard did not hug her back. My youngest sister does not lavish affection on him although they do carry on some rather interesting, if one-sided, conversations about their mutual enemy, the cat.

Friends of my parents pretend that they don't see Snoopy, politely ignoring what they consider sloppy housekeeping on my mother's part. On the contrary, it was she who put him there, and when she proudly draws attention to his presence the women coo like Barbara and think, "How quaint" and their husbands mutter an embarrassed, "Well, isn't that nice."

The only person who gave a completely sincere reaction was my current beau Marc who stalked into the house, stopped, curled his lip, gave Snoopy his best Jonathan Brewster stare and haughtily said "How gauche can you get!" Alas, poor Marc, you and all the others will never observe Snoopy's credo "To dance is to live; to live is to dance." There are very few dancers in my world.

hugs it, this piece of cardboard. (laughs) Those are two extremes and my mother had a suggestion, "Well, what about the adults who walk in and pretend not to see it?" and that might be interesting.

This business about writing about my grandmother, it would have been better if I had come last week because it was sort of fresh on my mind to do it then. But, I don't know, this Snoopy might be interesting if I could think of enough examples. Yeah, I think I'll write about that. Now, did you want me to start writing?

Now the problem is how to start it. I could say that I walked into the house one evening after work and there it was sitting in the middle of the living room. Or else, I could say something like, it's going to sound like a third grade introduction, but something about, "Can you imagine our surprise when we received a three foot by three foot cardboard packing thing in the mail?" That's also not too good a start. I have to think of how to begin the thing. You could say that it's not the ordinary thing to have in your living room and people don't expect to see it. Uh, you could say something about "one of the last things that people would expect to find in our," yeah, I could say, "people in a," no, "in a living room such as ours with the oak," what is it, I think it's walnut-paneled "walnut-paneled entranceway and shelves and book" yeah, "and book shelves lining the walls, almost the last thing one would expect to find would be a two-foot-high cardboard cut-out of Snoopy, the Peanuts dog. However, in the A——'s house just about anything is possible." (laughing) I think I can start like that.

Let's see, does this pen write, yeah (4 secs. pause) *One of the last things* (16 secs. pause [writing]) *someone would expect to find in a* now wait, to say, to get "in our living room," I'm now describing the living room. I either put "a," I could say, "our living room with its walnut-paneled entranceway and book-lined walls," but that's kind of a, I don't like the construction. I use it too much, I think. Then to put the height, some sort of hyphenated adjectives in front of "living room," that might be too awkward. *One of the last things one would expect to find in our,* (4 secs. pause) this thing about our living room, there are more books and magazines there, (laughing) that's no, really not so many books because there are boxes of books in the basement. There are only about two walls of books. There are magazines galore. Now, let's see, how could I say that?

One of the last things someone would expect to find, but if I say anything about there being magazines all over the place you are going to get an idea of disorder. Well that's partly true but it's not part of composition. *One of the last things someone would expect to find in our walnut-lined entrance in the* (11 secs, pause [writing]) I'm not going to say *our living room* in the first sentence. I'm going to say *in the living room,* yeah, "in the living room" (9 secs. pause) "in the living room," oh, I know, I love my hyphenated adjectives, *in the living room with walnut-paneled book-lined walls* [writing] *one of the last things someone would expect to find,* "one of the last things" is sort of a cliché phrase but it's okay, it's *one of the last things someone would expect to find in the living room with walnut-paneled book-lined walls,* that sort of gives you a sedate atmosphere. "Book-lined walls" would be, I've, I've, I've split some, I've made some sort of error here, expect to find then in a blah, blah, blah, that long sentence then would be awkward, *walnut-paneled, a* (7 secs. pause) *very large cardboard statue of Snoopy, the Peanuts dog.* Something about "but in our living room" (13 secs. pause [writing]) just make a short sentence to relieve after all of that (12 secs. pause [writing]) *anything is possible* (3 secs. pause) something about it is hard to describe the utter bliss that is on this dog's face if you've ever seen the picture of the dancing where they had "to live is to dance, to dance is to live." Eh, I know, I could sort of give the setting instead of saying it is hard to describe. I could say "he dances in front," "he dances," he's right in the middle of the living room by the doorway. "He dances in front of the living room." *He dances,* (16 secs. pause) *he dances with an expression of utter bliss on his face.* [writing] I could say "smack in the middle of the" let's see. *He dances with the expression of utter bliss on his face directly in the path of anyone* [writing] yes this is going to be good *entering the front door.* [writing] Now this gives me a tie-in to relate in different people's reactions. Hm, that's pretty clever, Lynn. "One of the last," I want to read this part over again, I think I might start a new paragraph. (20 secs. pause) Now I think I can put something also in that sentence about "he dances," I might make it *he dances with an expression of utter bliss on his face his arms held open in greeting, directly in the path* (3 secs. pause) et cetera. (3 secs. pause) *Directly in the path of anyone entering the front door.* Hm, let's see. (9 secs. pause [writing]) "Whether one," uhm, "whether an arrival would respond to his invitation to the dance," *whether a guest or a visitor would,* [writing] let's see. "Whether a guest" "visitor," what's a good word? Something about "entrance," but "entrance" isn't good because that's like entering school. "Whether a visitor," just about all I can think of. "Caller," that's trite. No, archaic. Uhm. "Visitor," "whether a visitor," no I don't think "whether a visitor responds to" because then I have nothing to finish the sentence with. Something about, I could just go right in saying he does—wait, uhm. Something, I have to get in the reactions of the people who walk in the front door. Now let's see (20 secs. pause) I've been reading over the sentence a couple of times and I still can't think of, something about "since he is unavoidable" [writing] yeah, that's right. Yeah, "since he is unavoidable all visitors to our house register some sort of reaction." "Since he is unavoidable, all visitors to our house register some sort of reaction." *Since he is unavoidable, all visitors to our house register some sort of reaction.* [10 secs. writing] Now that sentence isn't finished. If you can put a period at the end of it, then it sort of leaves you hanging. (6 secs. pause) "Must register some sort of reaction." "Must register some sort of reaction." Then I can go into examples. I don't, it's not smooth but I might be able to figure something out later. "Some sort of reaction." Uhm, (3 secs. pause) I could say something about it might be a reflection on the personalities of the people, the way they react to this dog, but then I'd have to go into this for every person, maybe it would just be better to stay on the surface, and just give what they say now. I want to start out with my girl friend who picked the thing up and hugged it or with this boy who sort of just yeah, (laughing) looked at it. Yeah, I could start with my girl friend Barbara since she responded in a positive manner and she just put her arms out and hugged the thing. Now let's see how can we say that? "Some sort of reaction."

"My girl friend," (10 secs. pause) "my girl friend Barbara in the true spirit of a dedicated Schultz fan" you could say. *My girl friend Barbara in the true,* [writing] I haven't said how this dog got to be there but I don't really think it's necessary. "My girl friend Barbara in the true," no no, no. (4 secs. pause) Yeah, now I can bring some, *my girl friend Barbara who also holds her arms open in greetings to the world responds who holds her arms,* [writing] yeah, instead of "also holds," instead of putting the emphasis there, you could say "who holds *her* arms," putting the emphasis on "her," underlined or something, I don't know. *My girl friend Barbara who holds her arms open in greeting to the world picked up Snoopy in all his cardboard cuddliness,* picked up Snoopy in all his stiff cardboard cuddliness "picked up Snoopy in all his stiff cardboard," leave out the "stiff," *cuddliness and hugged him.* [writing] She sort of, she was. She remembered the motto that when the Snoopy sweatshirts had Snoopy this same picture of Snoopy. "My girl friend Barbara who holds her arms in greeting," I think we also. "My girl friend Barbara who holds her arms open in greetings" "also" has to be in there, because the people might not, whoever reads this might not catch the continuity. Not "picked," I can't say "picked up and hugged him" it's too much, "embraced Snoopy" instead of "picked up," because she had to pick him up to embrace him. (4 secs. pause) "And she sort of cooed, 'Isn't he sweet?'" you know like that. (20 secs. pause [writing]) Even, yeah, even my youngest sister doesn't hug him (9 secs. pause [writing]) although. *Even my youngest sister does not hug him although she does carry on,* now something in between those two sentences, about I thought Barbara's reaction was a little extreme. "Since he's unavoidable, all visitors to our home must register some sort of reaction." "My girl friend Barbara, who also holds her arms open to the world, embraced Snoopy in all his cardboard cuddliness and cooed, 'Isn't he sweet?'" I felt this was just too much. Now this is going to the reaction to the other kid. Something about how cardboard does not. I was afraid it would break, yeah, I was afraid his arms would break off. (7 secs. pause) No, "the cardboard did not respond," "did not" *The cardboard did not hug her back.* [writing] *Even my littlest, even my youngest sister does not* now "hug" was used in the sentence before. I also used "embraced," there's another word, *does not lavish her affections on him, although she does.* Yeah. *Lavish affection on him although she does carry on some rather interesting* (7 secs. pause [writing]) *if one-sided* (14 secs. pause) *conversations about their mutual enemy, the cat.* The cat does not like Snoopy, she jumps at it and knocks it over. Now Debbie does like the cat but it's just nice to put some little tie-in here between her and Snoopy. If she saw this she would probably be very mad because she is very fond of the cat. "Even though my other sister does not lavish affection on him, although she does carry on some rather interesting if one-sided conversations, about their mutual enemy, the cat." Now I could talk about what the cat does. Perhaps the cat realizes that Snoopy is a dog and therefore dislikes him, or perhaps she's jealous that people seem to pay more attention to him when they walk in the door. But she sort of gives it a whack with her paw when she walks by. My father pretends to hate the cat. . . . when he walks by [he'll] stamp his foot. That's sort of what the cat's doing to Snoopy. That's an entirely different story.

(laughing) I think I can just drop the cat and now if I can find I could say something about "next on our scale of affections." (10 secs. pause) I don't think even my youngest sister, maybe perhaps just "my youngest sister does not lavish affection on him although she does carry on some rather interesting if one-sided," although *they do,* [writing] instead of "she does." *They do carry on some rather interesting if one-sided conversations about their mutual enemy the cat. At the opposite end, at the opposite end, at the opposite end of our* [writes] Now if I said "reaction scale" you'd get reaction to something in chemistry and you'd. This really negative reaction won't be as strong as when Barbara picks the thing up and she just laps it and loves it. I don't know if I can say that. The cat, (9 secs. pause) *one of my current boy friends,* I could, yeah, just the cat, I have to use something in the sentence before as a tie-in, with the rest of the, I have to use something as a tie-in with the rest of it. (13 secs. pause)

What I want to say is something like, "one of my current boy friends regards Snoopy with disgust." No, I think maybe I can start out an entirely new chapter without bothering about connecting it with the paragraph before. Uhm. (8 secs. pause) Now these two kids, Barbara and Marc, are friends, they've been friends for some years. I could say, they do sort of have opposite personalities. This is interesting considering they're friends. My girl friend Barbara, now let's see, all this business about Barbara. (8 secs. pause) *Marc, one of Barbara's friends, has, Marc, one of my friends.* I could just say, just start out say. (10 secs. pause) Oh, I know. I can talk about the adults or friends of my parents usually. *Friends of my parents,* [writes] I think faster than I write. I was already writing "usually" when I forgot "of my parents." *Friends of my parents pretend they don't see Snoopy politely ignoring what they consider to be sloppy housekeeping on my mother's part. On the contrary, it was she who put him there and when she probably draws attention to this presence the woman coo like Barbara and the men* (6 secs. pause [writing]) *the men mutter an embarrassed, "Well, isn't that nice?"* They don't say "quaintly," you can tell that's what they're thinking. (14 secs. pause) "Coo like Barbara," yeah, I think I should put in something about thinking "how quaint." Oh, I know. *The women coo like Barbara and think "How quaint" their husbands mutter an embarrassed, "Well, isn't that nice?"* [writing] Now I want to end it up with something about, I could tie-in these men's reactions, to bring in Marc's and then wrap it up. Uhm, (10 secs. pause) There's something awkward about the construction of the sentence before. If I read the whole thing through, the whole paragraph.

"Friends of my parents pretend they don't see Snoopy, politely ignoring what they consider to be sloppy," now this "what they consider to be" might be too wordy, "what they consider," leave out the "to be." *Friends of my parents pretend that they don't see Snoopy, politely ignoring what they consider sloppy housekeeping,* leave out the "to be," it's too much. "What they consider to be sloppy housekeeping on my mother's part. On the contrary, it was she who put him there and when she probably draws attention to his presence, the women coo like Barbara and think, 'How quaint.' Their husbands mutter an," I need another "and" in there. "And their husbands mutter an embarrassed, 'Well, isn't that nice?'" *The only,* yeah, *the only person who gave a completely sincere reaction was my current* [writes] I use the word "beau" because I want to set the stage. "My current beau Marc who," he sorta, when he walks he sorta like 'Here I am, aren't you glad that I'm here?' He sorta stalked into the house. (5 secs. pause) *He stalked into the house, stopped* (5 secs. pause) *curled his lip, gave Snoopy his best Jonathan Brewster,* [writing] now I don't know if you, Jonathan Brewster is the Frankenstein nephew in *Arsenic and Old Lace.* He played him in a play, it was excellent, "gave Snoopy his best Jonathan Brewster," now a look that is threatening. What's that called? "His best Jonathan Brewster" I can do it. "His best Jonathan Brewster," I could say "stare." The only person, what is it? I can't think of the word, when you look at, really a threatening look like, it's a fantastic thing. I can't think of the word now. "His best Jonathan Brewster." (5 secs. pause) Hm, "the only person who gave a completely sincere reaction was my current beau, Marc, who stalked into the house, stopped, curls his lip, gave Snoopy his best Jonathan Brewster," I'll have to say "snare"—"stare," I mean—(5 secs. pause [writing]) and, "said," "muttered," those aren't good words, *gave Snoopy his best Jonathan Brewster stare* and now he said it sarcastically but this is what, this kid, he covers up everything by saying things sarcastically. *He gave Snoopy his best Jonathan Brewster stare and sarcastically said,* no not sarcastically. *And said,* it's the only word I can think of. [writes] *He said, "Lynn,"* no, I'm not going to put my name in it, I think it's too many names in there and we'll get all mixed up. *"How gauche can you get?"* [writes] "Gauche," I guess that's it. *Alas,* [writes] oh this is good, I like this. I can end it right here. *Alas, poor Marc,* (11 secs. pause) *he will never believe Snoopy's credo, "to dance is to live, to live is to dance."* (6 secs. pause) "Snoopy's credo 'to dance.'" (4 secs. pause [writes]) Now I don't know. That's not really an ending. You will never believe Snoopy's, (4 secs. pause reading over the last paragraph.) I have to think of a better ending (10 secs. pause) "Alas, poor Marc," "alas, poor Hamlet"—no, "alas, poor Yorick" (laughs) "will never observe Snoopy's credo." "You and all the others will never observe Snoopy's credo" and I can sort of end. 'To live is to dance,' I'm not completely satisfied with the ending. 'To dance is to live, to live is to dance.' Uh. "There are a very few dancers." (7 secs. pause) *Alas, poor Marc, you and all the others will never observe Snoopy's credo, "To dance is to live, to live is to dance." There are very few dancers in my world* [writes] That's good, well not good, but it's okay. Now title, (7 secs. pause) " 'Terpsichordean' means 'to dance.' " you could say "terpsichordean greeting" but I don't like to so much. (3 secs. pause) Yeah, is it "terps *e*" or "*i*"? O. K. that's about it.

Investigator: Really, just one question, at the beginning you contemplated a number of possible topics and then decided against all but one of them. You suggested that the reason for not choosing your grandmother was that it was really not as fresh as it might have been last week. Were there other reasons for not using that topic or for not using the others that you originally contemplated?

Lynn: No, I don't think so, not particularly pertaining to my grandmother since she lives on the north side, I don't see her that much and over the week, the intervening week, since she was at our house last weekend, the

Snoopy thing's come and so as I said, I've been preoccupied with other things. The Snoopy thing is easier to write about. And if I would have been here last week, I probably could have done it because I wouldn't have had so many distractions in between. The Snoopy thing is the easiest thing to write on because you can almost make up what you want to say, you can sort of predict the reactions, although these are true. It's not too hard. To write about my grandmother one thing that really struck me was when she would sit down in a chair she would sort of almost fall into it and my mother would sort of watch her when she was going up the stairs because they don't have stairs at her house, and this had never occurred to me before that she was rather old. And it would be kind of hard to formulate an entire theme. If I would have perhaps seen her again this week or, I didn't see too many old people on the buses going downtown either which would have •
given me some insight. No this is the easiest thing to write about. The business about writing about one of the boys that I'm going out with sort of limited. It's nothing very original or interesting. To me it's interesting.

Investigator: So originality and appeal were two reasons for choosing this?

Lynn: I don't know if it's really original because I'm sure people have written compositions on similar themes but its sort of nice using composition, yeah, it has more universality than writing about. Oh, I'm sure everybody has had a boyfriend at one time in their life but this is just more interesting. It's very easy to get trite when you're talking about. It's very easy to write like I said before one of these short stories in a fashion magazine.

Investigator: For next time would you think about and/or write something in what might be called imaginative writing, this is more descriptive expository. If you wish or a short story poem and some of the other people who have been doing this have preferred not to write this in my presence rather to write it on their own, keeping a record of what they're doing because in some cases it might take longer and then calling me whenever it's ready and then coming in and we sort of review the writing of it. If you prefer, or if you want to write it in my presence, you can. You could do it either way.

Lynn: No, I think I'd rather write it at home and I might be able to write it on one of these other two topics I was talking about write it at home short story, because short stories involve a good plot and I find it hard to invent plots and would be easier.

Investigator: Is next Tuesday at 10:00 all right?

Lynn: Next Wednesday.

NOTES

Introduction

1. D. Gordon Rohman, "Pre-Writing: The Stage of Discovery in the Writing Process," *College Composition and Communication* (May 1965), p. 106.
2. See, for example, "Obsessions and Phobias: Their Psychical Mechanisms and Their Aetiology" (1895) and "Further Remarks on the Defence Neuro-Psychoses" (1896), in *Collected Papers*, Vol. I. Authorized translation under the supervision of Joan Riviere (New York: Basic Books, Inc., 1959).
3. Henry Meckel, "Research on Teaching Composition and Literature," *Handbook of Research on Teaching*, ed. N.L. Gage, p. 972. Copyright by American Educational Research Association, Washington, D.C.
4. Richard Braddock, Richard Lloyd-Jones, and Lowell Schoer, *Research in Written Composition*, pp. 31-32.
5. "Recent Measures in Language Development," speech, National Conference on Research in English, Chicago, 1965.

Chapter 1

1. Peter de Vries, Interview from *Counterpoint*, compiled and edited by Roy Newquist, p. 147.
2. Exemplars of writers' accounts in these modes, in the order mentioned in the text, are: Virginia Woolf, *A Writer's Diary, Being Extracts from the Diary of Virginia Woolf*, ed. Leonard Woolf; Katherine Mansfield, *Journal of Katherine Mansfield*, ed. J. Middleton Murry; Gerard Manley Hopkins, *The Note-books and Papers of Gerard Manley Hopkins*, ed. Humphry House; John Keats, *The Selected Letters of John Keats*, ed. Lionel Trilling; Henry James, *The Art of the Novel, Critical Prefaces by Henry James*, ed. Richard P. Blackmuir; Elizabeth Bowen, "Notes on Making a Novel," *Collected Impressions;* E.M. Forster, *Aspects of the Novel;* F. Scott Fitzgerald, *The Crack-Up*, ed. Edmund Wilson, pp. 69-84; J. Paul Sartre, *The Words*, trans. Bernard Frechtman; *Writers at Work: The Paris Review Interviews I*, ed. Malcolm Cowley; Dylan Thomas, "An Evening with Dylan Thomas," Caedmon Recording No. 1157; "Creative Person, W. H. Auden," National Educational Television (NET) telecast, April 17, 1967.
3. T.S. Eliot, "East Coker," *Four Quartets*. Copyright 1943 by Harcourt Brace Jovanovich, Inc. and Faber and Faber Ltd. Used by permission.
4. D. H. Lawrence, *Studies in Classic American Literature*, p. 11.
5. John Ciardi, Interview from *Counterpoint*, compiled and edited by Roy Newquist, pp. 122-23. Copyright 1964 by Rand McNally & Company. Used by permission.
6. H.E.F. Donohue, *Conversations with Nelson Algren; The Journals of Arnold Bennett*, ed. Frank Swinnerton; Joseph Conrad, *The Mirror of the Sea* and *A Personal Record*, ed. Morton Dauwen Zabel; Simone de Beauvoir, *The Prime of Life*, trans. Peter Green; Guy de Maupassant, "Preface to *Pierre et Jean*," *The Life Work of Henry Rene Guy de Maupassant;* F. Scott Fitzgerald, *The Crack-Up;* E.M. Forster, *Writers at Work: The Paris Review Interviews*, II; Andre Gide, *The Journals of Andre Gide*, trans. Justin O'Brien; John Keats, *Selected Letters;*

Norman Mailer, *Advertisements for Myself;* Katherine Mansfield, *Journal;* Jean Paul Sartre, *The Words;* Robert Louis Stevenson, *Essays in the Art of Writing;* Leo Tolstoi, *Talks with Tolstoi: Tolstoi and His Problems,* trans. Aylmer Maude; Mark Van Doren, *Autobiography;* H.G. Wells, *Experiment in Autobiography; Discoveries and Conclusions of a Very Ordinary Brain (Since 1866).*
7. Virginia Woolf, *A Writer's Diary,* ed. Leonard Woolf, p. 21. Used by permission of Harcourt Brace Jovanovich, the Hogarth Press, and the author's literary estate.
8. *Ibid.,* p. 25.
9. *The Letters of Gerard Manley Hopkins to Robert Bridges,* ed. Claude Colleer Abbott.
10. *The Letters of Thomas Wolfe,* ed. Maxwell Perkins.
11. Malcolm Cowley, *The Faulkner-Cowley File: Letters and Memories, 1944-1962.*
12. Jerome Beaty, *Middlemarch, From Notebook to Novel: A Study of George Eliot's Creative Method.* Copyright 1960 by University of Illinois. Used by permission.
13. *Ibid.,* pp. 110-11.
14. *Ibid.,* p. 123.
15. *Ibid,* p. 125.
16. Janet Emig, "The Uses of the Unconscious in Composing," *College Composition and Communication* (February 1964), p. 11.
17. From *Classical Rhetoric for the Modern Student* by Edward P.J. Corbett, p. 566. Copyright © 1965 by Oxford University Press, Inc. Used by permission.
18. *Essays on Rhetoric,* ed. Dudley Bailey, p. 82.
19. Graham Wallas, *The Art of Thought,* pp. 79-81. Copyright 1926 by Harcourt Brace Jovanovich. Used by permission.
20. Malcolm Cowley, *Writers at Work, The Paris Review Interviews.* Copyright 1961 by the Viking Press, Inc. and Martin Secker & Warburg Limited. Used by permission.
21. R.N. Wilson, "Poetic Creativity, Process and Personality," *Psychiatry* (1954), pp. 163-76.
22. L.S. Kubie, *Neurotic Distortion of the Creative Process,* pp. 44-45.
23. Jerome Bruner, "The Conditions of Creativity," *On Knowing: Essays for the Left Hand.*
24. *Ibid.*
25. Arthur Koestler, *The Act of Creation,* p. 38.
26. *Ibid.,* p. 95.
27. Anthony Tovatt and Ebert L. Miller, "The Sound of Writing," *Research in the Teaching of English* (Fall 1967), pp. 182-83.
28. *Ibid.,* pp. 187-88.
29. D. Gordon Rohman and Albert O. Wiecke, *Pre-Writing: The Construction and Application of Models for Concept Formation in Writing,* Michigan State University, 1964, USOE Cooperative Research Project No. 2174, p. 103.
30. *Ibid.,* p. 30.
31. *Ibid.,* p. 181.
32. John E. Warriner, Joseph Mersand, and Francis Griffith, *English Grammar and Composition, 11,* pp. 379-80. Copyright 1958 by Harcourt Brace Jovanovich. Used by permission.
33. John Hyde Preston, "A Conversation," *Atlantic Monthly* (August 1935), p. 189. Reprinted by permission of Harold Ober Associates Incorporated. Copyright 1935 by John Hyde Preston.
34. Respondents to a questionnaire devised and distributed July 1964 by Janet Emig were: Max Bluestone, University of Massachusetts, Boston; Reuben Brower,

Harvard University; Jerome Bruner, Harvard University; John B. Carroll, Harvard University; John Ciardi, poet, Poetry Editor, *Saturday Review;* Kenneth Lynn, Harvard University; Raven I. McDavid, University of Chicago; Harold Martin, President, Union College; Theodore Morrison, novelist, Harvard University; Henry Olds, Harvard Graduate School of Education; James K. Robinson, University of Cincinnati; Israel Scheffler, Harvard University; Clifford Shipton, Director, American Antiquarian Society, Worcester, Massachusetts; B.F. Skinner, Harvard University; Priscilla Tyler, Harvard University; Mark Van Doren, poet, Columbia University.

35. Eileen Bassing, Interview from *Counterpoint*, compiled and edited by Roy Newquist. Copyright 1964 by Rand McNally & Company. Used by permission.

Chapter 3

1. M.A.K. Halliday, Angus McIntosh, and Peter Strevens, *The Linguistic Sciences and Language Teaching*, p. 77.
2. Wilson, "Poetic Creativity," p. 167.
3. Harold Rosen, Lecture, NDEA Institute in English Composition, University of Chicago, July 1968.
4. Research of James Britton, Nancy Martin, and Harold Rosen, Institute of Education, University of London.
5. Wilson, "Poetic Creativity," p. 168.
6. Jerome Bruner, "Teaching a Native Language," *Toward a Theory of Instruction*, p. 103. Copyright 1966 by Belknap Press of Harvard University Press. Used by permission.
7. For an interesting discussion of the ordering of elements, see Francis Christensen's "A Generative Rhetoric of the Sentence," *Notes Toward a New Rhetoric*, pp. 1-22.
8. Richard Ohmann, "Generative Grammars and the Concept of Literary Style," *Word* (1964), p. 431.
9. *Ibid.*, p. 433.
10. *Ibid.*
11. The terminology employed in this section is, for the most part, borrowed from studies of hesitation phenomena, particularly from "Hesitation Phenomena in Spontaneous English Speech" by Howard Maclay and Charles E. Osgood, *Readings in the Psychology of Language*, pp. 305-24.

Chapter 4

1. Leon A. Jakobovits, "Rhetoric and Stylistics: Some Basic Issues in the Analysis of Discourse," *College Composition and Communication* (December 1969), p. 325.
2. Ohmann, "Generative Grammars," p. 431.
3. *Ibid.*, p. 433.
4. Paul C. Rodgers, Jr., "A Discourse-centered Rhetoric of the Paragraph," *College Composition and Communication* (February 1966), p. 5.
5. Frieda Goldman-Eisler, "Discussion and Further Comments," *New Directions in the Study of Language*, ed. Eric H. Lenneberg, p. 120.
6. George A. Miller, "Some Psychological Studies of Grammar," *Readings in the Psychology of Language*, ed. Leon A. Jakobovits and Murray S. Miron, p. 212.

Chapter 5

1. See, for example, the discussion by George A. Miller in *Language and Communication*, pp. 157-58.

2. Dolores Durkin, *Children Who Read Early*, p. 136.
3. Others who have noted this phenomenon include Duane C. Nichols, "The Five-Paragraph Essay: An Attempt to Articulate," and Arnold Lazarus, "On the Teaching of Composition," in *Teaching High School Composition*, ed. Gary Tate and Edward P.J. Corbett, pp. 247-54 and pp. 219-28.

Chapter 7

1. Kellogg Hunt, *Grammatical Structures Written at Three Grade Levels;* and Roy C. O'Donnell, William S. Griffin, and Raymond C. Norris, *Syntax of Kindergarten and Elementary School Children: A Transformational Analysis.*
2. Kellogg Hunt et al., *An Instrument to Measure Syntactic Maturity.*
3. See the accounts, for example, in Sybil Marshall, *An Experiment in Education* and David Holbrook, *The Secret Places: Essays on Imaginative Work in English Teaching and on the Culture of the Child.*
4. From *The Secret Places* by David Holbrook, p. 69. Copyright © by David Holbrook. Used by permission of the University of Alabama Press.

BIBLIOGRAPHY

ALLEN, WALTER ERNEST, ed. *Writers on Writing*. London: Phoenix House, 1948.

ANDERSON, SHERWOOD. *A Story Teller's Story*. New York: Viking Press, 1927.

ANGENE, LESTER E. "Proposals for the Conduct of Written-Composition Activities in the Secondary School Inherent in an Analysis of the Language Composition Act." Unpublished doctoral dissertation, Ohio State University, 1955.

ARIETI, SILVANO. *The Intrapsychic Self: Feeling, Cognition and Creativity in Health and Mental Illness*. New York: Basic Books, 1967.

ARISTOTLE. *Rhetoric*. Translated and edited by Lane Cooper. New York: Appleton-Century-Crofts, 1960.

ARNHEIM, RUDOLPH, et al. *Poets at Work: Essays Based on the Modern Poetry Collection at the Lockwood Memorial Library, University of Buffalo*. New York: Harcourt Brace Jovanovich, 1948.

AUDEN, W.H. *The Sea and the Mirror*. New York: Random House, 1944.

BAILEY, DUDLEY, ed. *Essays on Rhetoric*. New York: Oxford University Press, 1965.

BARRON, FRANK. "The Psychology of Imagination." *Scientific American* (1958), pp. 151-60.

BEACH, JOSEPH WARREN. *The Making of the Auden Canon*. Minneapolis: University of Minnesota Press, 1957.

BEATY, JEROME. *Middlemarch from Notebook to Novel: A Study of George Eliot's Creative Method*. Urbana, Ill.: University of Illinois Press, 1960.

BEAUVOIR DE, SIMONE. *Memoirs of a Dutiful Daughter*. Translated by James Kirkup. London: A. Deutsch, Weidenfeld and Nicolson, 1959.

BEAUVOIR DE, SIMONE. *The Prime of Life*. Translated by Peter Green. Cleveland, Ohio: World Publishing, 1962.

BENNETT, ARNOLD. *Journal of Things New and Old*. Garden City, New York: Doubleday, Doran and Co., 1930.

BENNETT, ARNOLD. *The Journals of Arnold Bennett*. Edited by Frank Swinnerton. London: Penguin Books, 1954.

BENNETT, ARNOLD. *The Truth about an Author*. Westminster, England: A. Constable and Co., 1903.

BENNETT, JOSEPHINE W. *The Evolution of "The Faerie Queene."* Chicago: University of Chicago Press, 1942.

BEREITER, CARL. "Verbal and Ideational Fluency in Able 10th Graders." *Journal of Educational Psychology* (1960), pp. 337-45.

BERRYMAN, JOHN. *Stephen Crane*. New York: Sloane, 1950.

BETTELHEIM, BRUNO. *The Empty Fortress: Infantile Autism and the Birth of the Self*. New York: Free Press, 1967.

BETTELHEIM, BRUNO. *The Informed Heart: Autonomy in a Mass Age*. Glencoe, Ill.: Free Press, 1960.

BETTELHEIM, BRUNO. *Love Is Not Enough: The Treatment of Emotionally Disturbed Children.* Glencoe, Ill.: Free Press, 1950.

BIBER, BARBARA. "Premature Structuring as a Deterrent to Creativity." *American Journal of Ortho-Psychiatry* (1959), pp. 280-90.

BLAIR, HUGH. *Lectures on Rhetoric and Belles-Lettres* (1783). Edited by Harold F. Harding. Carbondale, Ill.: Southern Illinois University Press, 1965.

BLOOM, BENJAMIN. *Stability and Change in Human Characteristics.* New York: John Wiley & Sons, 1964.

BODER, D.P. "The Adjective-Verb Quotient." *The Psychological Record* (1940), pp. 309-43.

BOOTH, WAYNE. *The Rhetoric of Fiction.* Chicago: University of Chicago Press, 1961.

BOWEN, CATHERINE DRINKER. *Biography: The Craft and the Calling.* Boston: Little Brown, 1969.

BOWEN, ELIZABETH. "Notes on Making a Novel." *Collected Impressions.* New York: Alfred A. Knopf, 1950.

BRADBURY, Ray. "At What Temperature Do Books Burn?" *New York Times* (November 13, 1966), p. D 11.

BRADDOCK, RICHARD, RICHARD LLOYD-JONES, and LOWELL SCHOER. *Research in Written Composition.* Urbana, Ill.: National Council of Teachers of English, 1963.

BRITTON, JAMES, ed. *Talking and Writing: A Handbook for English Teachers.* London: Methuen, 1967.

BRUNER, JEROME. *On Knowing: Essays for the Left Hand.* Cambridge, Mass.: Harvard University Press, 1962.

BRUNER, JEROME. *Toward a Theory of Instruction.* Cambridge, Mass.: Belknap Press of Harvard University Press, 1966.

BUCKLEY, JEROME H. *Tennyson: The Growth of a Poet.* Cambridge, Mass.: Harvard University Press, 1960.

BUEHLER, KARL. "On Thought Connections." *Organization and Pathology of Thought.* Edited and translated by David Rapaport. New York: Columbia University Press, 1951, pp. 39-57.

BUTT, JOHN, and KATHLEEN TILLOTSON. *Dickens at Work.* London: Methuen, 1957.

BUXTON, EARL W. "An Experiment to Test the Effects of Writing Frequency and Guided Practice upon Students' Skill in Written Expression." Unpublished doctoral dissertation, Stanford University, 1958.

CALDER, GRACE J. *The Writing of "Past and Present," a Study of Carlyle's Manuscripts.* New Haven, Conn.: Yale University Press, 1949.

CALITRI, CHARLES J. "A Structure for Teaching the Language Arts." *Harvard Educational Review* (Fall 1965), pp. 481-91.

CAMPBELL, GEORGE. *The Philosophy of Rhetoric* (1776). Edited by Lloyd F. Bitzer. Carbondale, Ill.: Southern Illinois University Press, 1963.

CAMUS, ALBERT. *Notebooks, 1942-1951.* Translated and annotated by Justin O'Brien. New York: Alfred A. Knopf, 1965.

CANE, MELVILLE. *Making a Poem: An Inquiry into the Creative Process.* New York: Harcourt Brace Jovanovich, 1953.

CARROLL, JOHN B. "Vectors of Prose Style." In Thomas A. Sebeok, ed.,

Style in Language. Cambridge, Mass.: MIT Press, 1960.

CATHER, WILLA. "The Novel Demeublé." *Not under Forty.* New York: Alfred A. Knopf, 1936.

CHRISTENSEN, FRANCIS. *Notes toward a New Rhetoric: 6 Essays for Teachers.* New York: Harper & Row, 1967.

CICERO. *De Oratore.* Books I and II. Translated by E.W. Sutton and H. Rackham. Book III. Translated by H. Rackham. 2 vols. Cambridge, Mass.: Loeb Classical Library, 1942.

CLANCY, JOSEPH P. "Literary Genres in Theory and Practice." *College English* (April 1967), pp. 486-95.

COLETTE. *The Vagabond.* Translated by Enid McLeod. New York: Farrar, Straus and Young, 1955.

COLVIN, S.S. "Invention versus Form in English Composition: An Indicative Study." *Pedagogical Seminary* (1902), pp. 393-421.

COLVIN, S.S., and I.F. MEYER. "Imaginative Elements in the Written Work of School Children." *Pedagogical Seminary* (1906), pp. 84-93.

CONNOLLY, FRANCIS X. *A Rhetoric Casebook.* New York: Harcourt Brace Jovanovich, 1953.

CONRAD, JOSEPH. *Conrad's Prefaces to His Works.* Edited by Edward Garnett. London: J.M. Dent, 1937.

CONRAD, JOSEPH. *The Mirror of the Sea* and *A Personal Record.* Edited by Morton Dauwen Zabel. Garden City, New York: Anchor Books, Doubleday, 1960.

CORBETT, EDWARD P.J. *Classical Rhetoric for the Modern Student.* New York: Oxford University Press, 1965.

COWLEY, MALCOLM. *The Faulkner-Cowley File: Letters and Memories, 1944-1962.* New York: Viking Press, 1966.

COWLEY, MALCOLM, ed. *Writers at Work: The Paris Review Interviews.* New York: Viking Press, 1958.

"The Creative Person: W.H. Auden." National Educational Television (NET) Telecast. April 17, 1968.

CREWS, FREDERICK. "Anaesthetic Criticism," Part I, *New York Review of Books* (February 26, 1970), pp. 31-35.

CREWS, FREDERICK. "Anaesthetic Criticism," Part II. *New York Review of Books.* (March 12, 1970), pp. 49-52.

DEWEY, JOHN. *Art as Experience* (1934). New York: G.P. Putnam's Sons, 1958.

DEWEY, JOHN. *How We Think.* New York: D.C. Heath and Co., 1933.

DONOHUE, H.E.F. *Conversations with Nelson Algren.* New York: Berkley Medallion Books, 1964.

DOSTOEVSKY, FYODOR. *The Notebooks for "Crime and Punishment."* Edited and translated by Edward Wasiolek. Chicago: University of Chicago Press, 1968.

DOSTOEVSKY, FYODOR. *The Notebooks for "The Idiot."* Edited by Edward Wasiolek; translated by Katherine Strelsky. Chicago: University of Chicago Press, 1967.

DURKIN, DOLORES. *Children Who Read Early: Two Longitudinal Studies.* New York: Teachers College Press, 1966.

ECKER, DAVID W. "The Artistic Process as Qualitative Problem Solving." In

Elliot W. Eisner and David W. Ecker, eds., *Readings in Art Education.* Waltham, Mass.: Blaisdell Publishing Co., 1966.

ELIOT, T.S. "East Coker." *Four Quartets.* London: Faber and Faber, 1960.

EMIG, JANET A. "Components of the Composing Process among Twelfth-Grade Writers." Unpublished doctoral dissertation, Harvard University, 1969.

EMIG, JANET A. "Planning Practices of Students and of Professional Writers." Working paper, Harvard Graduate School of Education, 1963.

EMIG, JANET A. "The Uses of the Unconscious in Composing." *College Composition and Communication* (February 1964), pp. 6-11.

FITZGERALD, F. SCOTT. *The Crack-Up.* Edited by Edmund Wilson. New Canaan, Conn.: New Directions, 1956.

FORSTER, E.M. *Aspects of the Novel.* New York: Harcourt Brace Jovanovich, 1927.

FREUD, SIGMUND. "The Relation of the Poet to Day-Dreaming" and "Leonardo da Vinci and a Memory of His Childhood." *Collected Papers.* Translated by Joan Riviere. New York: Basic Books, 1956.

GETZELS, JACOB W., and MIHALY CSIKSZENTMIHALYI. *Creative Thinking in Art Students: An Exploratory Study.* Chicago: University of Chicago Press, 1965.

GETZELS, JACOB W., and PHILIP W. JACKSON. *Creativity and Intelligence: Explorations with Gifted Students.* London, New York: John Wiley & Sons, 1962.

GIDE, ANDRE. *The Journals of André Gide.* Translated by Justin O'Brien. New York: Alfred A. Knopf, 1947.

GILBERT, A.H. *On the Composition of "Paradise Lost": A Study of the Ordering and Insertion of Material.* New York: Octagon Books, 1966.

GODSCHALK, FREDERICK I., FRANCES SWINEFORD, and WILLIAM E. COFFMAN. *The Measurement of Writing Ability.* New York: College Entrance Examination Board, 1966.

GOLDMAN-EISLER, FRIEDA. "Discussion and Further Comments." In Eric H. Lenneberg, ed., *New Directions in the Study of Language.* Cambridge, Mass.: MIT Press, 1964.

GORDON, W.J.J. *Synectics: The Development of Creative Capacity.* New York: Harper & Row, 1961.

GRAVES, ROBERT. *On English Poetry: Being an Irregular Approach to the Psychology of This Art, from Evidence Mainly Subjective.* New York: Alfred A. Knopf, 1922.

GUILFORD, J.P. "The Structure of Intellect." *Psychological Bulletin* (1956), pp. 267-93.

GUILFORD, J.P. "Three Faces of Intellect." *American Psychologist* (1959), pp. 469-79.

HADAMARD, JACQUES. *An Essay on the Psychology of Invention in the Mathematical Field.* New York: Dover Press, 1954.

HALLIDAY, M.A.K., ANGUS MCINTOSH, and PETER STREVENS. *The Linguistic Sciences and Language Teaching.* Bloomington, Ind.: Indiana University Press, 1964.

HEBB, DONALD O. *The Organization of Behavior: A Neuropsychological Theory.* New York: John Wiley & Sons, 1949.

HIGGINSON, F.H. *Anna Livia Plurabelle: The Making of a Chapter*. Minneapolis: University of Minnesota Press, 1960.

HILDICK, EDMUND WALLACE. *Word for Word: A Study of Authors' Alterations with Exercises*. London: Faber and Faber, 1965.

HOLBROOK, DAVID. *English for the Rejected: Training Literacy in the Lower Streams of the Secondary School*. Cambridge, England: Cambridge University Press, 1964.

HOLBROOK, DAVID. *The Secret Places: Essays on Imaginative Work in English Teaching and on the Culture of the Child*. University, Ala.: University of Alabama Press, 1965.

HOPKINS, GERARD MANLEY. *The Letters of Gerard Manley Hopkins to Robert Bridges*. Edited by Claude Colleer Abbott. London: Oxford University Press, 1935.

HOPKINS, GERARD MANLEY. *The Note-books and Papers of Gerard Manley Hopkins*. Edited by Humphry House. New York: Oxford University Press, 1937.

HOUSMAN, A.E. *The Name and Nature of Poetry*. New York: Cambridge University Press, 1933.

HOWELL, WILLIAM S. *Logic and Rhetoric in England, 1500-1700*. Princeton, N.J.: Princeton University Press, 1956.

HOWELLS, W.D. "Novel-writing and Novel-reading: An Impersonal Explanation." *Howells and James: A Double Billing*. Edited by William M. Gibson. New York: New York Public Library, 1958.

HUNT, KELLOGG W. *Grammatical Structures Written at Three Grade Levels*. Urbana, Ill.: National Council of Teachers of English, 1965.

HUNT, KELLOGG W., et al. *An Instrument to Measure Syntactic Maturity* (Preliminary Version). Tallahassee: Florida State University, 1968.

IKER, HOWARD P., and NORMAN HARWAY. "A Computer Approach towards the Analysis of Content." *Behavioral Science* (April 1965), pp. 173-82.

JACKSON, PHILIP W. *Life in Classrooms*. New York: Holt, Rinehart and Winston, 1968.

JACKSON, PHILIP W., and SAMUEL MESSICK. "The Person, the Product, and the Response: Conceptual Problems in the Assessment of Creativity." In Jerome Kagan, ed., *Creativity and Learning*. Boston: Beacon Press, 1967.

JAKOBOVITS, LEON. "Rhetoric and Stylistics: Some Basic Issues in the Analysis of Discourse." *College Composition and Communication* (December 1969), pp. 314-28.

JAKOBSON, ROMAN. "From the Viewpoint of Linguistics: Closing Statement: Linguistics and Poetics." In Thomas A. Sebeok, ed., *Style in Language*. Cambridge, Mass.: MIT Press, 1960.

JAMES, HENRY. *The Art of the Novel: Critical Prefaces by Henry James*. New York: Charles Scribner & Sons, 1962.

JAMES, HENRY. *Hawthorne* (1879). Ithaca, N.Y.: Cornell University Press, 1967.

JONES, RICHARD M. *Fantasy and Feeling in Education*. New York: New York University Press, 1968.

JOYCE, JAMES. *Letters of James Joyce*. Edited by Stuart Gilbert. New York: Viking Press, 1957.

JOYCE, JAMES. *A Portrait of the Artist as a Young Man: Text, Criticism and Notes.* Edited by Chester G. Anderson. New York: Viking Press, 1968.

KEATS, JOHN. *The Selected Letters of John Keats.* Edited by Lionel Trilling. New York: Farrar, Straus and Young, 1951.

KINNEAVY, JAMES E. "The Basic Aims of Discourse." *College Composition and Communication* (December 1969), pp. 297-304.

KIPLING, RUDYARD. *Something of Myself for My Friends Known and Unknown.* New York: Doubleday, 1937.

KLEIN, GEORGE S. "Consciousness in Psychoanalytic Theory: Some Implications for Current Research in Perception." In R.M. Jones, ed., *Contemporary Educational Psychology: Selected Readings.* New York: Harper & Row, 1967.

KOESTLER, ARTHUR. *The Act of Creation.* New York: Macmillan, 1964.

KOHL, HERBERT. *36 Children.* New York: New American Library, 1967.

KRIS, ERNST. *Psychoanalytic Explorations in Art.* New York: International Universities Press, 1952.

KUBIE, LAWRENCE S. *Neurotic Distortion of the Creative Process.* Lawrence, Kan.: University of Kansas Press, 1958.

LAWRENCE, D.H. *The Letters of D.H. Lawrence.* Edited by Aldous Huxley. New York: Viking Press, 1932.

LAWRENCE, D.H. *Studies in Classic American Literature.* London: Thomas Seltzer, 1923.

LAZARUS, ARNOLD. "On the Teaching of Composition." In Gary Tate and Edward P.J. Corbett, eds., *Teaching High School Composition.* New York: Oxford University Press, 1970.

LOWELL, AMY. *Poetry and Poets.* Boston: Houghton Mifflin, 1930.

LOWE, LEE FRANK. "Writers on Learning to Write." *English Journal* (October 1964), pp. 488-95.

LOWES, JOHN LIVINGSTON. *The Road to Xanadu: A Study in the Ways of the Imagination.* New York: Houghton Mifflin, 1927.

LYMAN, ROLLO L. *Summary of Investigations Relating to Grammar, Language, and Composition.* Chicago: University of Chicago, 1929.

McCORMACK, THOMAS, ed. *Afterwords: Novelists on Their Novels.* New York: Harper & Row, 1968.

MACLAY, HOWARD, and CHARLES E. OSGOOD. "Hesitation Phenomena in Spontaneous English Speech." In Leon A. Jakobovits and Murray S. Miron, eds., *Readings in the Psychology of Language.* Englewood Cliffs, N.J.: Prentice-Hall, 1967.

MAILER, NORMAN. *Advertisements for Myself.* New York: G.P. Putnam's Sons, 1960.

MALRAUX, ANDRE. *The Voices of Silence.* Translated by Stuart Gilbert. Garden City, N.Y.: Doubleday, 1953.

MANN, THOMAS. "Tonio Kröger." *Stories of Three Decades.* Translated by H.T. Lowe-Porter. New York: Alfred A. Knopf, 1948.

MANSFIELD, KATHERINE. *Journal of Katherine Mansfield.* Edited by J. Middleton Murry. Rome: Albatross, 1950.

MARSHALL, SYBIL. *An Experiment in Education.* New York: Cambridge University Press, 1963.

MARTIN, HAROLD, RICHARD OHMANN, and JAMES WHEATLEY. *The Logic and Rhetoric of Exposition.* New York: Holt, Rinehart and Winston, 1969.

MASLOW, ABRAHAM H. "Peak Experiences as Acute Identity Experiences." *American Journal of Psychoanalysis* (1961), pp. 254-60.

MAUD, RALPH. *The Notebooks of Dylan Thomas.* New Canaan, Conn.: New Directions, 1967.

MAUGHAM, W. SOMERSET. *The Summing-Up.* New York: Literary Guild of America, 1938.

MAUPASSANT DE, GUY. "Preface to *Pierre et Jean.*" *The Life Work of Henry Rene Guy de Maupassant.* Akron, Ohio: St. Drustan Society, 1903.

MECKEL, HENRY C. "Research on Teaching Composition and Literature." In N.L. Gage, ed., *Handbook of Research on Teaching.* Chicago: Rand McNally and Co., 1963.

MELLON, JOHN C. *Transformational Sentence-Combining: A Method for Enhancing the Development of Syntactic Fluency in English Composition.* Urbana, Ill.: National Council of Teachers of English, 1969.

MILLER, GEORGE A. *Language and Communication.* New York: McGraw-Hill, 1951.

MILLER, GEORGE A., EUGENE GALANTER, and KARL H. PRIBRAM. *Plans and the Structure of Behavior.* New York: Henry Holt, 1960.

MILLER, GEORGE A. "Some Psychological Studies of Grammar." In Leon A. Jakobovits and Murray S. Miron, eds., *Readings in the Psychology of Language.* Englewood Cliffs, N.J.: Prentice-Hall, 1967.

MILNE, A.A. *Autobiography.* New York. E.P. Dutton, 1939.

MOFFETT, JAMES. *Teaching the Universe of Discourse.* Boston: Houghton Mifflin, 1968.

MOSTELLER, FREDERICK, and DAVID L. WALLACE. *Inference and Disputed Authorship: The Federalist.* Reading, Mass.: Addison-Wesley Publishing Co., 1964.

MURRAY, DONALD M. *A Writer Teaches Writing: A Practical Method of Teaching Composition.* Boston: Houghton Mifflin, 1968.

MURRY, J.M. *The Problem of Style.* London: Oxford University Press, 1922.

NEMEROV, HOWARD. *Journal of the Fictive Life.* New Brunswick, N.J.: Rutgers University Press, 1965.

NEWQUIST, ROY, ed. *Counterpoint.* Chicago: Rand McNally and Co., 1964.

NICHOLS, DUANE C. "The Five-Paragraph Essay: An Attempt to Articulate." In Gary Tate and Edward P.J. Corbett, eds., *Teaching High School Composition.* New York: Oxford University Press, 1970.

NIETZSCHE, F. "Composition of *Thus Spake Zarathustra.*" *Ecce Homo.* Translated by Clifton Fadiman. New York: Random House, 1927.

O'DONNELL, BERNARD. *An Analysis of Prose Style to Determine Authorship.* The Hague: Mouton, 1970.

O'DONNELL, ROY C., WILLIAM S. GRIFFIN, and RAYMOND C. NORRIS. *Syntax of Kindergarten and Elementary School Children: A Transformational Analysis.* Urbana, Ill.: National Council of Teachers of English, 1967.

OHMANN, RICHARD. "Generative Grammars and the Concept of Literary Style." *Word* (December 1964), pp. 423-39.

PAGE, ELLIS B., and DIETER H. PAULUS. *The Analysis of Essays by Computer.* Storrs: University of Connecticut, 1968.

PARKINSON, THOMAS. *W.B. Yeats: The Later Poetry*. Berkeley: University of California Press, 1964.

PATRICK, CATHERINE. "Creative Thoughts in Poets." *Archives of Psychology* (April 1935).

PATRICK, CATHERINE. *What Is Creative Thinking?* New York: Philosophy Library, Inc., 1955.

PIAGET, JEAN. *The Language and Thought of the Child*. Translated by Marjorie Gabain. New York: World Publishing Co., 1955.

PIERCY, JOSEPHINE, ed. *Modern Writers at Work*. New York: Macmillan, 1930.

PLATO, *Phaedrus, Ion, Gorgias, Symposium, with Passages from the Republic and Laws*. Translated by Lane Cooper. New York: Oxford University Press, 1948.

POE, EDGAR ALLAN. "The Philosophy of Composition." In Robert L. Hough, ed., *Literary Criticism of Edgar Allan Poe*. Lincoln: University of Nebraska Press, 1965.

POLANYI, MICHAEL. *The Tacit Dimension*. Garden City, N.Y.: Doubleday, 1966.

POINCARE, HENRI. "Mathematical Creation." *The Foundations of Science* (1913). Translated by George Bruce Halsted. New York: Science Press, 1946.

POPE, ALEXANDER. *Epistle to Bathurst*. Edited by Earl R. Wasserman. Baltimore: Johns Hopkins University Press, 1960.

PRESTON, JOHN HYDE. "A Conversation." *Atlantic Monthly* (August 1935), pp. 187-94.

PRIESTLEY, J.B. *Rain upon Godshill*. New York: Harper Bros., 1939.

QUINTILIAN. *Institutio Oratoria*. Translated by H.E. Butler. 4 vols. London: W. Heinemann, 1920-22 (Loeb Classical Library).

RADER, R.W. *Tennyson's Maud: The Biographical Genesis*. Berkeley: University of California Press, 1963.

RIDLEY, M.R. *Keats' Craftsmanship: A Study in Poetic Development*. Lincoln: University of Nebraska Press, 1963.

RILKE, RAINER MARIA. *The Notebook of Malte Laurids Brigge*. Translated by M.D. Herter Norton. New York: W.W. Norton, 1949.

ROBINSON, HELEN M. *Why Pupils Fail in Reading: A Study of Causes and Remedial Treatment*. Chicago: University of Chicago Press, 1946.

ROCKAS, LEO. *Modes of Rhetoric*. New York: St. Martin's Press, 1964.

RODGERS, PAUL C., JR. "A Discourse-centered Rhetoric of the Paragraph." *College Composition and Communication* (February 1966), p. 5.

ROGERS, NEVILLE. *Shelley at Work: A Critical Inquiry*. Oxford: Clarendon Press, 1956.

ROHMAN, D. GORDON. "Pre-Writing: The Stage of Discovery in the Writing Process." *College Composition and Communication* (May 1965), p. 106.

ROHMAN, D. GORDON, and ALBERT O. WIECKE. *Pre-Writing: The Construction and Application of Models for Concept Formation in Writing*. East Lansing, Mich.: Michigan State University, 1964. USOE Cooperative Research Project No. 2174.

ROSEN, HAROLD, JAMES BRITTON, AND NANCY MARTIN. "Abilities to Write." *NEW Education* (October 1966).

SARTRE, JEAN-PAUL. *Being and Nothingness: An Essay on Phenomenological Ontology.* Translated and with an introduction by Hazel E. Barnes. New York: Washington Square Press, 1966.

SARTRE, JEAN-PAUL. *The Words.* Translated by Bernard Frechtman. New York: G. Braziller, 1964.

SCHACHTEL, ERNEST. *Metamorphosis: On the Development of Affect, Perception, Attention and Memory.* New York: Basic Books, 1959.

SCHNEIDER, DANIEL E. *The Psychoanalyst and the Artist.* New York: New American Library of World Literature, 1962.

SCOTT, NATHAN A., JR., ed. *Four Ways of Modern Poetry.* Richmond, Va.: John Knox Press, 1965.

SHERIDAN, RICHARD BRINDLEY. *The Rivals.* Edited by Richard B. Purdy from the Larpent manuscript. Oxford, England: Clarendon Press, 1935.

SILBERER, HERBERT. "On Symbol-Formation." *Organization and Pathology of Thought.* Edited by David Rapaport. New York: Columbia University Press, 1951.

SMITH, BARBARA HERRNSTEIN. *Poetic Closure: A Study of How Poems End.* Chicago: University of Chicago Press, 1968.

SMITH, RODNEY P. *Creativity in the English Program.* Urbana, Ill.: National Council of Teachers of English, Educational Resources Information Center: Clearinghouse on the Teaching of English, 1970.

SPENDER, STEPHEN. *The Making of a Poem.* London: H. Hamilton, 1955.

SQUIRE, JAMES R. *The Responses of Adolescents While Reading Four Short Stories.* Urbana, Ill.: National Council of Teachers of English, 1964.

STALLWORTHY, JON. *Between the Lines: Yeats' Poetry in the Making.* New York: Oxford University Press, 1963.

STEMMLER, ANNE O. "Reading of Highly Creative versus Highly Intelligent Secondary Students." Unpublished doctoral dissertation, University of Chicago, 1968.

STEVENSON, ROBERT LOUIS. *Essays in the Art of Writing.* London: Chatto and Windus, 1905.

STONE, PHILIP, ROBERT BOLES, et al. "The General Inquirer. . . ." *Behavioral Science* (1962), pp. 3-16.

SWAIN, EMELIZA. "Conscious Thought Processes Used in the Interpretation of Reading Materials." Unpublished doctoral dissertation, University of Chicago, 1953.

TCHEKHOV, ANTON. *The Life and Letters of Anton Tchekhov.* Translated and edited by S.S. Koteliansky and Philip Tomlinson. New York: H. Doran Co., 1925.

THOMAS, DYLAN. *An Evening with Dylan Thomas.* Caedmon Recording No. 1157.

THOMAS, DYLAN. *Quite Early One Morning.* New York: New Directions, 1954.

TOLSTOI, LEO. *Talks with Tolstoi: Tolstoi and His Problems.* Translated by Aylmer Maude. London: G. Richards, 1904.

TORRANCE, E. PAUL. *Guiding Creative Talent.* Englewood Cliffs, N.J.: Prentice-Hall, Inc., 1962.

TOVATT, ANTHONY. "Oral-Aural-Visual Stimuli for Teaching Composition." *English Journal* (March 1965), pp. 191-95.

Tovatt, Anthony, and Ebert L. Miller. "The Sound of Writing." *Research in the Teaching of English* (Fall 1967), pp. 176-89.

Valery, Paul. *The Art of Poetry.* Translated by D. Folliot with an introduction by T.S. Eliot. *The Collected Works.* Vol. 8. New York: Random House, 1958.

Valery, Paul. *L'Introduction à la Poétique.* Paris: Gallimard, 1938.

Van Bruggen, John A. "Factors Affecting Regularity of the Flow of Words during Written Composition." *Journal of Experimental Education* (December 1946).

Van Doren, Mark. *Autobiography.* New York: Harcourt Brace Jovanovich, 1958.

Vygotsky, Lev. *Thought and Language.* Translated by E. Hanfman and G. Vakar. Cambridge, Mass.: MIT Press, 1962.

Walker, John. *The Teacher's Assistant in English Composition; or Easy Rules for Writing Themes and Composing Exercises on Subjects Proper for the Improvement of Youth of Both Sexes at School. To Which Are Added, Hints for Correcting and Improving Juvenile Composition.* Boston: 1803.

Wallas, Graham. *The Art of Thought.* New York: Harcourt Brace Jovanovich, 1926.

Warriner, John E., Joseph Mersand, and Francis Griffith. *English Grammar and Composition, 11.* New York: Harcourt Brace Jovanovich, 1958.

Watson, James D. *The Double Helix: A Personal Account of the Structure of DNA.* New York: Atheneum, 1968.

Weismann, Donald L. *Language and Visual Form: The Personal Record of a Dual Creative Process.* Austin: University of Texas Press, 1968.

Wells, H.G. *Experiment in Autobiography; Discoveries and Conclusions of a Very Ordinary Brain (Since 1866).* New York: Macmillan, 1934.

Wharton, Edith. *A Backward Glance.* New York: D. Appleton-Century Co., 1934.

Whately, Richard. *Elements of Rhetoric* (1828). Edited by Douglas Ehninger. Carbondale, Ill.: Southern Illinois University Press, 1963.

Williams, Raymond. *The Long Revolution.* London: Chatto & Windus, 1961.

Williams, Tennessee. "Playwright as Individual: A Conversation with Tennessee Williams." *The Playbill for Hello, Dolly!* Edited by Walter Wazer, 1966.

Wilson, R.N. "Poetic Creativity, Process and Personality." *Psychiatry* (1954), pp. 163-76.

Wolfe, Thomas. *The Letters of Thomas Wolfe.* Edited by Maxwell Perkins. New York: Charles Scribner's Sons, 1938.

Wolfe, Thomas. *The Story of a Novel.* New York: Charles Scribner's Sons, 1949.

Wolfe, Tom. "What If He Is Right?" *The Pump House Gang.* New York: Farrar, Straus and Giroux, 1968.

Woolf, Virginia. *A Writer's Diary, Being Extracts from the Diary of Virginia Woolf.* Edited by Leonard Woolf. New York: Harcourt Brace Jovanovich, 1954.

WORDSWORTH, WILLIAM. "Preface to Lyrical Ballads." *Lyrical Ballads by Wordsworth and Coleridge.* Edited by R.L. Brett and A.R. Jones. London: Methuen, 1963.

WORDSWORTH, WILLIAM. *The Prelude; or Growth of a Poet's Mind.* Edited from the manuscripts by Ernest de Selincourt. Oxford, England: Clarendon Press, second edition, 1959.

Writers at Work: The Paris Review Interviews, second series. Introduced by Van Wyck Brooks. New York: Viking Press, 1963.

Writers at Work: The Paris Review Interviews, third series. Introduced by Alfred Kazin. New York: Viking Press, 1967.